PRAISE FOR
HIGH STEPPERS, FALLEN ANGELS, AND LOLLIPOPS

"Fascinating reading of Wall Street slang and anecdotes. Recommended for anyone interested in how the players think and speak."

—David Dreman,
Dreman Value Management

"A delightful book for a three-hour plane ride and for your office bookshelf."

—Robert Kirby,
Capital Guardian Trust Co.

"As a stock market and word addict, I found the book a perfect fix."

—Michael Metz,
Oppenheimer & Co.

"Laugh if you want to—and you will—but *High Steppers, Fallen Angels, and Lollipops* gives you serious inside information on lighthearted moments in the pursuit of money . . . that ought to be mine."

—Ross L. Muir,
Lazard Frères & Co.

"This book is great fun and makes you aware of just how much jargon we take for granted."

—Dee Osborn,
Shearson Asset Management

"A fascinating lexicon of Wall Street anecdotes and slang, past and present. Diverting reading for financiers and laymen alike."

—Calvert Dooman,
J.&W. Seligman & Co.

High Steppers, Fallen Angels, and Lollipops

WALL STREET SLANG

Kathleen Odean

Foreword by Leonard Silk

AN OWL BOOK

HENRY HOLT AND COMPANY

NEW YORK

Copyright © 1988 by Kathleen Odean
All rights reserved, including the right to reproduce this
book or portions thereof in any form.
Published by Henry Holt and Company, Inc.,
115 West 18 Street, New York, New York 10011.
Published in Canada by Fitzhenry & Whiteside Limited,
195 Allstate Parkway, Markham, Ontario L3R 4T8.

Library of Congress Cataloging-in-Publication Data
Odean, Kathleen.
High steppers, fallen angels, and lollipops : Wall Street slang /
Kathleen Odean ; foreword by Leonard Silk.—1st Owl book ed.
p.   cm.
Reprint. Originally published: New York, Dodd, Mead, 1988.
"An Owl book."
Bibliography: p.
Includes index.
ISBN 0-8050-1038-6 (pbk.)
1. Brokers—New York (N.Y.)—Language (New words, slang, etc.)
2. English language—New York (N.Y.)—Slang.   3. New York Stock
Exchange—Slang.   4. Americanisms—New York (N.Y.)   5. Stock-
exchange—Slang.   6. Wall Street—Slang.   7. Speculation—Slang.
I. Title.
[PE3727.B76034   1989]
332.6'014—dc19   89-1894   CIP

Henry Holt books are available at special discounts
for bulk purchases for sales promotions, premiums,
fund-raising, or educational use. Special editions
or book excerpts can also be created to specification.

For details contact:

Special Sales Director
Henry Holt and Company, Inc.
115 West 18th Street
New York, New York 10011

First published in hardcover by Dodd, Mead & Company, Inc.
in 1988.
First Owl Book Edition—1989

Printed in the United States of America
1   3   5   7   9   10   8   6   4   2

TO MY PARENTS,
WILLIAM AND EILEEN ODEAN

Contents

Foreword   ix

Acknowledgments   xi

Introduction   1

1. From High Steppers to Alligator Spreads:
   Stocks, Bonds, and Other Tools of the Trade   5

2. Mad Dog, Kitty Cat, and Marilyn Monroe:
   Nicknames for Stocks and Bonds   26

3. Suckers, Scalpers, and the Smart Money Boys:
   People in the Market   46

4. Kings and Queens, Wizards and Witches:
   Nicknames for People   64

5. Buy Low, Sell High: Playing the Market   85

6. The Fantasy World of Corporate Takeovers   102

7. Swindles and Scandals   120

8. Exchanges and Brokerages of the
   Gold-Paved Street   142

9. Blue Mondays and Black Fridays:
   Nicknames of Events and Times   163

10. Inflated Images and Underlying Doubts:
    Analysis of Metaphors   180

Notes	193
Bibliography	198
Index	203

Foreword
by Leonard Silk

Once upon a time, when I was a soldier, what a delight it was, what a crazy kind of privilege, to call a fellow G.I. a goldbrick, a sad sack—really a sad sack of shit—a goofoff, a fuckup. Why was military slang so obscene? I guess because, in what was then a man's world (for the most part, still is), G.I. slang was useful for proving that you could live in a world without women, turn a lousy situation into a joke, maybe even squeeze some fun out of it. The rough talk proved that you could handle almost anything, that you belonged.

In this fascinating book, Kathleen Odean demonstrates that Wall Street slang is as rich as military slang and serves a like purpose: to separate the men from the boys and the women from the girls, insiders from outsiders, winners from losers; to make the risks, the frustrations, and the losses bearable; to make speculation—a hard way to live—bearable, if not exactly respectable; to make so hazardous a way of life a joke on yourself, not just on others; to provide, in its own gross way, the consolation of philosophy—but not much of a philosophy, when you come right down to it.

The slang of Wall Street is full of cheap wisdom, rules for making money that fail when bubbles burst ("When the paddy wagon comes, they take the good girls with the bad girls," "When in doubt, get out," "The easiest way to go broke is to be right too soon," "Don't sell America short," "Cut short your losses, let your profits run," "Sell 'em. Sell 'em. They're not worth anything.") Some of the wisdom of Wall Street has a defined ancestor. J. P. Morgan the elder said don't short America; David Ricardo, the economist, said let profits run (how long?); and Bernard E. Smith coined "Sell 'em." But most slang is an emanation of the air of Wall Street. It seems to be born spontaneously all over the Street, created, like the newspaper, by the news.

Nobody knows all the slang of Wall Street—nobody could; new slang is always being born, and old slang is always dying. Slang is like fashion: its point and its value is its freshness. It needs to be changed to prove you're still sharp. If slang endures and is transmogrified into a cliché, who wants it? Some old Wall Street slang survives but at the cost of losing its humor: There's nothing funny about a bull or a bear, a bargain hunter or bottom-fisher, and poison pills and greenmail are already losing their wittiness.

When Wall Street loses its savor, who will restore its saltiness? The Federal Reserve Board? The Treasury? The White House?

None of the above. We can't wait that long. If the fun is to return to Wall Street, the wits who work there will have to restore it. Their irreverent slang will keep alive the spirit we need to survive. The boom had its language and so will the bust.

Ms. Odean's tour through the language of Wall Street, laterally and backward through time, reminds us that this, too, will pass. As Sophie Tucker, the vaudevillian, used to say, "I've been rich, and I've been poor, and richer is better." But poor is okay, if you don't take it too seriously.

Acknowledgments

In researching the book, I have interviewed brokers and traders across the country about their slang; I thank all of them for their time and enthusiasm, with special thanks to Mitchell Asch, Dave Becker, Skip Jones, and Joe Stamler and his friends at the New York Stock Exchange. I also gathered material on current and historical slang from newspapers, magazines, and books, drawing on the outstanding libraries at the University of California at Berkeley. The NYSE Archives also proved useful, and I would like to thank archivist Steven Wheeler for his help. Since the book grew out of a master's thesis in folklore at U.C. Berkeley, I wish to thank Professors Alan Dundes and John Lindow, and my colleagues Mary Koske and Marcy Williams. The late Peter Tamony offered me insights from his years of research in slang, for which I am grateful. I also thank my agent Richard Balkin and my editor Cynthia Vartan. A special debt of gratitude goes to Earl Cheit for all his help, and to June and Dave Cheit for reading and commenting on various chapters. Above all, I thank my husband Ross Cheit, who contributed numerous newspaper clippings and, more important, offered me unfailing encouragement throughout the project.

Introduction

Slang flourishes on Wall Street today as it has for more than two hundred years. In that time, Wall Streeters have created an entire lexicon, coining colorful words and phrases to describe themselves and their world. "Every shade and flavor of speculation [is] generally nicknamed and gibbeted with an epithet," wrote James Medbery about Wall Street in 1871, an observation that still holds true.

Wall Street slang encompasses words that are centuries old but still used, and others that fade after a few years, a few decades, or longer. *Bull* and *bear* originated in England in the 1700s and have retained their popularity; *customer's man,* heard constantly in the 1920s, has been replaced by newer terms. For every phrase that falls from use, others enter the slang. In the last ten years, Wall Streeters have added *pin-striped pork bellies, jellyroll spreads,* and a host of slang for hostile takeovers, from *poison pills* to *greenmail.* No one can predict for certain which terms will survive and which will fade.

What conditions cause a body of slang to survive and thrive in the stock market? A description of the exchange floor from the 1878 book *Men and Idioms of Wall Street* gives several clues:

> Any one looking on the brokers from the visitors' gallery, on a busy day, would think he had entered a human bee-hive. The jargon and gesticulations of the brokers, the shouts of the messenger boys, mingled with the unintelligible din from a thousand voices, presents a scene of confusion which can scarcely be described. The stranger would almost believe himself in a mad-house.

According to experts, favorable conditions for slang are "crowding and excitement, and artificial life," an apt description of an exchange floor in 1868 and today. Because emotions ride high when large amounts of money are at stake, Wall Streeters welcome any momentary diversion such as a colorful piece of slang or a joke to relieve the tension. The irreverence of slang, which turns important institutional investors into *elephants* and customers into *barefoot pilgrims,* injects humor into otherwise humorless situations.

The description of the "human bee-hive" with its "thousand voices" highlights another condition favorable to slang: the stock market's oral nature. Slang needs the spoken word in order to survive, and no place depends more on the spoken word than Wall Street. Brokers spend all day on the telephone with customers, traders shout and chat on trading floors, and investment bankers clinch deals at long-winded lunches; thus, catchy new words pass quickly from one Wall Streeter to another. (Besides slang, they share jargon, such as *P/E ratio* and *capital redemption yield,* terms that, unlike slang, are technical and not metaphorical.)

But only the slang that serves a purpose—adding humor, filling a gap in the language, expressing a shared emotion—gets passed on. Many would-be slang terms fall by the wayside because their appeal is weak and they don't contribute enough. As Carl Sandburg so well described it, "Slang is language which takes off its coat, spits on its hands—and goes to work."

Slang goes to work by painting pictures through metaphor, adding a sense of solidity to the abstract business of Wall Street, which lacks a physical product. With its figures of speech, slang supplies the concrete images for the world of trading. In the chapters that follow, slang terms for the heart of the business—the stocks, bonds, and other instruments of trading—are discussed first, including a chapter on nicknames for stocks and bonds, perhaps the wittiest words in the lexicon. Chapters Three and Four focus on the people who inhabit Wall Street today and those who did in the past. Chapter Five looks at slang for the techniques of buying and selling, and Chapter Six brings together the words and images in the new world of hostile takeovers. Chapter Seven deals with the swindles and scandals related to stock market trading, an area where the underworld and its slang overlap with Wall Street. The next two chapters delve into the history of the Street and its slang, describing places—exchanges and brokerages—and events, from *Blue Mondays* to *October Massacres.*

The final chapter explores the meaning of the slang through analyzing its metaphors, because metaphors draw comparisons and make evaluations. Every time Wall Streeters come up with a slang expression, they make a comment—often critical or irreverent—about the person, object, or event described. They reveal how they view themselves, their customers, and the market.

Through expressing shared values, the slang unifies the group. Familiarity with the latest expressions identifies those "in the know," while it mystifies and excludes outsiders. The same function is served by other folklore that thrives in the oral environment of the Street—jokes, anecdotes, legends, and proverbs shared by Wall Streeters. These appear often in the following pages to illustrate slang expressions or explain a concept about Wall Street; like slang—which is a form of folk speech—they reveal what Wall Streeters choose to talk about and pass down through the years.

Although Wall Streeters as a group share a body of slang and other folklore traditions, no one person will know all the slang in this book. The phrase "Wall Street" encompasses not just a few blocks in Manhattan, but a range of financial markets and institutions across the country, made up of many small, insular worlds. While everyone will know *Big Board* and *blue chip,* only certain

Wall Streeters will recognize *strangles, lollipops, lobby lizards,* or **Washtubs.** Even those who know Wall Street best will be surprised at the richness of the language and lore assembled in the following pages, and at how much they have to say about life on the Street.

1

From High Steppers to Alligator Spreads: Stocks, Bonds, and Other Tools of the Trade

CASTING SPELLS

Speculation is the romance of trade, and casts contempt upon all its sober realities. It renders the stock-jobber a magician, and the [stock] exchange a region of enchantment.

—Washington Irving

Through the magic of slang, Wall Street has cast its spell again and again to enchant investors. The romantic language, dispensing with sober reality, transforms an ordinary stock into a **glamour stock,** a **high-flier,** or a **pale blue chip.** A bond becomes a **flower** or is decked out with **bells and whistles.** Playing down its present mediocrity, a broker hints at great things in the future from a **growth** or **performance stock.** In a joke they tell, brokers laugh at their own tendency to paint a rosy picture of the future:

There was a gal who got married three times, but she was still a virgin. The first time she married an older guy and he couldn't

5

do it. Then she married a gay, and he wouldn't do it. Finally she married a stockbroker and all he did was sit on the edge of the bed and tell her how great everything was going to be.

But while the brokers plead guilty to exaggeration, they can point an accusing finger at their clients, who dearly love to hear how great everything is going to be. A cartoon that once appeared in *The Wall Street Journal* shows a woman telling her broker: "I was hoping you could suggest a highly speculative stock that's never failed to pay a dividend."

In the 1930s, facetious advice from brokers to "Buy Balloon Common—it always goes up!" sent gullible, greedy customers scurrying to the stock tables, looking for the imaginary stock whose name sums up the speculator's dream: a stock that will rise like a hot-air balloon and never come down.

Speculators' dreams fill the history of the market. In the 1800s, the public "took a fancy to" certain high-priced stocks that had a tendency to fluctuate, often due to market manipulation. Wall Street called these **fancy stocks** or **fancies,** about which market observer Philip Hone recorded in his diary in 1837:

> Within the last week many descriptions of what are called "fancy stocks" were inflated, by the progress of bubble-blowing, to prices double and quadruple those of the previous week . . . This inflated state of things lasted three days, and then came the reverse which always follows these high-pressure operations. All of a sudden stocks fell back nearly to the place where the speculation found them; the sellers became buyers, pocketed their gains, and laughed at their dupes.[1]

The fancies that fell became known as **traps,** since they had been part of a trap set by the big operators; by 1871, the slang word had fallen out of use, and was described by one writer as "almost obsolete."[2]

In the 1920s, speculators fell in love with **high steppers,** slang for fashionable stocks as well as for fashionably dressed people. One group of these high-steppers, the airline stocks, skyrocketed in popularity after Lindbergh's flight to Paris. Caught up in the excitement, investors blindly bought any stock that appeared to be connected with planes—including the Atlantic coast railroad named Seaboard Airlines, whose stock rallied along with the airlines.

While some investors follow the fashions, others seek a *sleeper,* a word used since at least 1929 to describe a promising stock whose value is not immediately apparent. Chances are that, before anyone realizes they are sleepers, these stocks trade inactively or, as the quip goes, "by appointment only." But, as business columnist Donald K. White wrote in 1983, "Nothing warms the heart of a securities analyst more than finding a 'sleeper' stock," and once discovered, they don't sleep long.[3] In general slang, *sleepers* are movies, books, or songs that unexpectedly become hits, or racehorses that unexpectedly win. Investors pray for the day when their sleepers will wake up and take off like a Derby winner.

The market of the late 1950s and the 1960s inspired extravagant slang for stocks. Market tipsters predicted that **wonder stocks** in exciting companies—some new, some newly recognized—would soar in price, touting stocks in bowling lanes, vending machines, hula hoops, and Davy Crockett hats. But despite airy predictions, only a few of the wonder companies, such as Xerox and Eastman Kodak, even survived.

Similar to wonder stocks, **glamour stocks** mesmerized the public starting in the 1960s. **Glamour,** which is still part of the Wall Street lexicon, implies a high price/earnings ratio and volatile performance in the market. In the 1960s and 1970s, the glamour stocks of industries that explored seemingly mysterious technology such as electronics or space exploration lured in the gullible. Investors sank more than $50,000 into OTC Enterprises, which, according to legend, promised them a trip to the moon in a "flying saucer." In recent years, genetic engineering stock has tempted investors, who drove the price of newly issued stock in Genentech from $35 to $89 on its first day in October 1980. It closed that day at $71.25 but its glamour diminished, until by March 1982 it had fallen to $17 a share.

Institutional investors once worshipped the **Nifty Fifty,** a group of glamour stocks and more traditional stocks, including such familiar names as American Express, J.C. Penny, Avon, and McDonalds. Some say that the "fifty" in this **Favorite Fifty** refers to fifty companies; others, to the stocks' selling prices of fifty times their earnings. Market pros in the 1980s occasionally harken the birth of a new Nifty Fifty or the return of the old, which fell from glory in 1974. (The name was parodied in the phrase **Shifty Thrifties,** a 1984 description of banks that took large credit risks.)

Traders also dubbed the original Nifty Fifty **Vestal Virgins** from the legendary six virgins who tended the sacred fire brought by Aeneas from Troy to Rome. The six served until age thirty, and any who lost her virginity before that age was buried alive. The market Vestal Virgins kept the fires of speculation burning, but some doubted their supposedly spotless reputation for long-term growth; as one market observer quipped, "They're not vestal virgins. In fact, they're out every night."[4]

Less exciting than Vestal Virgins are the **growth stocks,** which sound like they will flourish until attaining their potential of high earnings. They pay few or no dividends, because the company plows profits back into the business. Many a stock that was promoted as a growth stock never grew, a fact captured in a *New Yorker* cartoon that shows a broker hiding under his desk while his colleague explains to an irate customer, "He'll be sorry he missed you. But I can assure you that at the time we *all* considered it a stock with strong growth possibilities." In the same vein, stocks dubbed **performance stocks** do not always put on the performance the investor is looking for—a spectacular rise in price. The idea of performance dominated the Street in the mid-1960s, when mutual funds called **performance funds** dazzled investors with talk about rapid appreciation.

Talk, the lifeline of Wall Street, often takes the form of **stories** that revolve around **story stocks.** Stories relate recent events or predict upcoming ones; they give more information than tips do but fall short of confirmed fact. In 1972, *Newsweek* ran an article on them that began, "It's silly season on Wall Street; forgetting the blood bath they took in 1969 and 1970, individual and institutional investors alike are running up the prices of dozens of speculative stocks with a 'story.' "[5] In the early 1980s, computer software provided alluring *concepts,* as stock market stories are also called, while during the recent merger mania, traders have been calling real or speculated takeover candidates *story stocks.* Although stories may be all that these stocks have going for them—and stories don't always come true—they do liven up an otherwise dead market.

"What's in a name?" Shakespeare asked in *Romeo and Juliet.* "That which we call a rose / By any other name would smell as sweet." In the stock market, the right name for a company as well as the right slang for a stock can produce the sweet smell of financial success. In 1960, Jack Dreyfus of the Dreyfus Fund explained it this way:

> Take a nice little company that's been making shoelaces for 40 years and sells at a respectable six times earnings ratio. Change the name from Shoelaces, Inc. to Electronics and Silicon Furth-Burners. In today's market, the words "electronics" and "silicon" are worth 15 times earnings. However, the real play comes from the word "furth-burners," which no one understands. A word that no one understands entitles you to double your entire score.[6]

And a character in George Goodman's 1959 novel *The Wheeler Dealers* mused:

> "You tell people this stock is solid, it's got assets good as Fort Knox, its market price is less than its assets alone, they'll give you a big yawn. *But* you change the name from Universal Widget to Universal Automated Jet Rocket Fuel Missile Computers, it'll go to 100 tomorrow morning. That's *romance.* You

get *romance* in there, you don't have to have earnings or dividends or assets or a company even—the *romance* alone'll make
'em buy it."[7]

Romance lures people into the market and keeps them coming
back. In the spirit of romance investors throw caution to the wind
and *take a flier* or, as they said in the 1940s, *fly high,* by buying
an extremely speculative stock. Like any gamble, the *flier* or *high-
flier,* as such a stock has been called since the late 1800s, may
crash to the earth shattering the romance—at least until the next
furth-burner or rocket fuel stock comes along.

Like a gambler at the nickel slot machine, a certain type of
investor cannot resist spending small amounts over and over in
hopes of one big payoff. Such investors suffer from *penny-stockitis,* an addiction to *penny stocks,* which cost less than a dollar a
share and usually prove worthless. Penny-stockitis spread like an
epidemic in the 1950s when high-pressure telephone salesmen
working in the U.S. peddled penny stock in Canadian uranium
mines, until the Securities and Exchange Commission (SEC)
cracked down on them.

Wall Street disdainfully regards most penny stocks as *cats and
dogs,* a popular phrase in use since 1879 to describe low-priced,
often worthless, speculative stocks. The single word *dog* also means
a worthless security, and the related *pup* meant a low-priced,
inactive stock during the 1940s and 1950s. Although a well-worn
market maxim cautions, "Good stocks recover, but cats and dogs
die," investors dream that their cats and dogs—sometimes dubbed
wildcat stocks—will turn into *blue chips.*

Blue chip stocks, whose claim to fame is that they are not
gambles, take their name, oddly enough, from poker, in which
the blue chips used for betting are the highest denomination, followed by red, then white. As early as 1904, Wall Streeters applied
the poker term to high-priced, dividend-producing stocks of rep-
utable corporations. Stability is the key to blue chips—which are
the antithesis of *yo-yo stocks* whose prices go madly up and down—
and it takes years for a stock to qualify for the blue chip social

register. The stock must be **seasoned,** that is, proven stable over time. Stocks that are getting their seasoning, apparently on their way to becoming blue chips, are dubbed **pale blue chips** or **white chips.**

Certain blue chips act as **bellwethers,** stocks that lead the way up in rallies or down in declines. Some Wall Streeters claim that by watching bellwethers such as General Motors an observer can predict market trends, a belief others dismiss as sheer nonsense. The expression comes from the world of farming, where bell-wethers are male goats or sheep that wear bells around their necks and lead the rest of the flock. (In the underworld, according to dictionaries of slang, **bellwether** refers to the leader of a mob.)

Not all stocks have promising names, yet **fallen angels** tempt some Wall Streeters more than glamour stocks do. **Fallen angels,** which was nineteenth-century British slang on the stock exchange for defaulters, harkens back to the Bible's "How art thou fallen from heaven, O Lucifer, son of the morning." The phrase now describes stocks or bonds that had reached success but then began to perform badly; in the case of bonds, their ratings go down. Investors hope these lowly securities will return to their lofty status and produce profits.

The illusionary **phantom stocks** and **ghost stocks** do not trade at all. Corporations bestow phantom stocks as a perquisite by listing in an executive's account imaginary shares that do not carry voting rights and may not be traded. They do earn dividends, and gain or lose value depending on the current market price. When a market player such as a brokerage firm trading for its own account sells stock short without owning or borrowing the underlying stock, the new buyer pays but receives nothing except ghost stock, that is, a promise that stock will be delivered.

A STOCK IS BORN

We ought to legalize horse racing in every state. Sure people will bet, but at least they get to see the horses run and you certainly can't see General Motors and General Electric and General Utility run when you bet on them.[8]

In this typically astute comment, Will Rogers pinpoints a key aspect of the stock market: it has no physical product, no horses to watch. Brokers peddle stock in companies they have never visited, which make products they have never used. Customers who buy stocks no longer receive stock certificates, once decorated with pretty pictures and ornate writing, to clutch in their hands. Now they receive only numbers on computer-generated statements.

Slang serves Wall Street by supplying the horses—visual images that lend form to the abstract market. **Cats and dogs** and **Vestal Virgins** paint pictures to give life to intangible numbers and colorless names. At the same time, slang expresses emotions that financial terms do not convey. When a broker speaks of "wonder stocks," the customer feels an excitement that "high price/earnings ratio" would not inspire. When a broker scoffs, "What a dog," it stings more than, "It's a worthless stock."

Wall Streeters have created equally concrete images to describe the issuing of new stocks, when a corporation offers stock for sale to the public in order to raise capital. Like a ship setting off on a voyage, an issue of stock is **set afloat** or **floated,** and the launching is called a **flotation.** Whatever the public does not buy remains in the market as **floating stock.** (The entire financial world seems to be an ocean filled with *floating* words: *floating assets, floating debt, floating capital, floating rate note, floater,* and many more.)

The investment bankers who prepare flotations announce the birth of an issue with a **tombstone,** which they place in newspapers and business periodicals. This staid boxed announcement lists the amount of stock offered, the price, and the underwriters and dealers who have it for sale. Due to strict regulations, tombstones may not use advertising techniques. The slang comes from printers who, starting around 1880, applied the label *tombstone-style* to any advertisement that looked like a monumental inscription.

Despite the lifeless appearance of the tombstones, Wall Streeters have fought bitterly over them, and slang has captured the hostility of those fights which concern *bracketing*—the order in which the ads list underwriters. Originally, the brackets had a set pattern: near the top under the co-managers' names came the major bracket, then the mezzanine bracket, followed by the sub-major bracket and the regional brackets for the least important. The bigger the underwriter's role in the offering, the higher the bracket, within which the list was alphabetical.

The Great Alphabet War of 1976 broke out when underwriting subsidiary Halsey Stuart added Bache, the name of its parent company, before its own to gain a higher place in the bracket's alphabetical order. A series of battles, each dubbed *The Battle of the Bulge,* have raged about the creation of a *bulge bracket* at the top of the tombstone. In the early 1970s, five underwriters succeeded in establishing such an exclusive placement in announcements of debt offerings, and since then they have edged toward a bulge for equity offerings. The firms excluded from the bulge take up arms not because of lost profits—for, according to *The Wall Street Journal*, "the economic stakes in the bracketing battle are slim"—but because of the loss of power and prestige.

Only professionals get stirred up over today's tombstones, but before the SEC was created, announcements of new issues contrived to raise the excitement level of buyers to a fever pitch. Clarence Saunders, owner of the Piggly-Wiggly company, went all out in his 1923 full-page ad:

> Opportunity! Opportunity!
> It knocks! It knocks! It knocks!
> Do you hear? Do you listen? Do you understand?
> Do you wait? Do you act now? . . .
> Why then, asks the skeptic, can CLARENCE SAUNDERS be so
>   generous to the public?

In those days, firms distributed *hot stuff,* propaganda that promoted an issue with little regard for the truth. The SEC has since set down rules that prohibit flashy and false advertising, and require "full disclosure" of pertinent facts in order for a company to issue stock. Before securities can be sold to the public, a corporation must register with the SEC, then wait a number of days determined by the agency. Called the *cooling-off period* or the *cooling period,* these days presumably give the prospective buyer time to recover from any initial surge of excitement and calmly read the prospectus, a printed compilation of the important facts.

Before the price is set for the issue, the underwriters usually print a *red herring,* a preliminary draft of the prospectus, which must carry a warning printed in red ink that indicates the information may be incomplete. Although folk etymology points to these vertically placed red lines as the origin of the slang term, it is more likely that red herring is borrowed from general slang, where it means "an action or issue meant to divert attention from the main question," the intent of many early prospectuses. (The general slang comes from hunting in which hunters "fault the hounds" by drawing a red herring—one that is dried, smoked, and salted—across a fox's path to destroy its scent and set the hounds astray.)

If the stock offering will be made on a continuing basis, as shares in an open-end investment company would be, the issuer files an *evergreen prospectus.* It remains on file, periodically updated to reflect changes in the corporation.

Although clearance of a company's prospectus by the SEC does not imply endorsement, this fact is lost on many investors. A joke that made the rounds after the 1934 Securities Exchange Act quipped that a person could organize a company to encourage people to jump off the Empire State Building, and if the prospectus was in order, the SEC would approve it. Then as now, *caveat emptor*—"Let the buyer beware"—ruled the market, leaving the customer to determine if the pertinent facts about the company add up to future profit or loss.

Once the offering is for sale, the market must *digest* it. If an issue does not sell well, it *overhangs* the market, *undigested.* If it sells quickly, Wall Streeters call it a *hot issue* or a *blowout,* and they say it has *gone out the window.* Usually a hot issue rises sharply in price soon after it comes on the market.

The opposite of undigested securities are **digested** ones, those firmly held by investors. During some periods in the market, new issues do not sell easily; they are not simply undigested but, as J. J. Hill jested about stocks around the turn of the century, downright "undigestible." At other times, new issues sell quickly and skyrocket in price as a result of the Wall Street illness **new issue-itis.** When this disease sweeps the market as it did in the late 1970s and early 1980s, new companies with no earnings (and sometimes no product) decide to **go public,** offering stock to the public for the first time, and find a ready market.

Wall Streeters have a joke that they update depending on what type of issue is creating fervor at the moment. This version pokes fun at underwriters of mining stocks:

> An underwriter goes to heaven and finds that the spot desig-
> nated for underwriters is already overcrowded. He tells St. Peter
> that, with the help of a soapbox, he could make room for him-
> self, and St. Peter obliges by setting up a soapbox by the under-
> writers' area. The newcomer gets up and starts to shout about a
> terrific new mine just discovered in hell, where they're already
> selling stock for it. The underwriters to a man jump out and
> rush out of heaven to get shares, and as St. Peter watches, the
> newcomer starts running out too. "I know why they're leaving,"
> says the saint. "But where are you going?" As the man runs past,
> he yells back, "Maybe there's some truth to the rumor!"

The **new issue fever** brings out the **free-riders,** speculators who immediately buy as much of a hot issue as possible without ac-tually depositing any money, then sell it at a profit if and when the price goes up, using part of the profit to pay for the initial purchase. The buyer rides the stock up for free. An earlier British relative of the free-rider was the **stag,** a bull interested only in buying new issues to make a quick profit, a practice called **stag-ging the market.** Free-riders don't always confine themselves to new issues. Sometimes they place a purchase order for a listed stock with one broker, without initial payment, and if the stock goes up, sell it through another broker, using the profits to pay the first broker. If the stock goes down, the free-rider may deny ever placing the purchase order or may catch a ride out of town.

Flippers are another breed that thrives on new issues. The practice of *flipping,* mainly the pastime of private money managers, consists of buying newly issued stock first thing in the morning and selling it at a profit after the first rise in price. The flippers get their large blocks of stock from the underwriters, who are pleased to do favors for those who generate big commissions.

During a stock offering, the underwriters may exercise a *green shoe option* which allows them to issue an additional ten percent of the stock under certain conditions. For the largest stock sale in history, *Ma Bell* put on a green shoe and exercised the option to sell 1.2 million shares beyond the initial 16.5 million. The name comes from Green Shoe Manufacturing, the company that initiated the option in the 1950s. (Another shoe in the financial world, *white shoe,* describes prestigious firms that project an Ivy League, WASP image and lord it over the less prestigious *black shoe* types.)

Throughout the market's history, an unscrupulous practice in issuing stock has been to *water* it, that is, to dilute the stock significantly by selling numerous extra shares without an increase in company assets. For example, specialists at the American Stock Exchange engineered the *watering* of Swan Finch stock by increasing the shares from 35,000 to 2,016,566 between 1954 and 1957. Wall Streeters attribute the slang term to a legend about Daniel Drew, who took pride in fooling customers in any market.

> Drew would get up early and drive his cattle to New York City, stopping just north of town. There he would spread salt out on the ground and let his cattle graze but not allow them to drink. By the time the animals reached the cattle pens at Twenty-third Street, they were crazy with thirst and drank until swollen. With this extra poundage, the cattle sold for prices beyond their worth.

More likely, the origin of *to water stock* has a simpler explanation, as offered in a 1911 financial guide:

> A certain amount of water may be put into a quart of pure milk, and a greater bulk of what appears to be milk will result,

but the amount of food matter has not been increased by the process.[9]

To legitimately create new offspring, a corporation may issue new shares to its stockholders as a **spin-off,** forming a new subsidiary corporation. Shareholders in the original company, the **parent company,** receive stock in the new family member in proportion to their holdings in the parent.

More family imagery occurs in the rankings of securities that a corporation issues: **junior** and **senior.** Owners of senior securities have first claim to a company's assets and earnings, while junior securities have a secondary claim. Bonds are usually senior to preferred stock, while common stock is junior to both.

Whereas free-riders seek the quick killing, other stockholders care most about dividends, the distributions of cash from a company's profits. A company **cuts the melon** when it distributes an unexpectedly high dividend, known as a **melon** or **plum.** One slang dictionary, which dates the expression to 1908, suggests that **melon-cutting** comes from the Chinese phrase "carving up the melon," used in the late nineteenth century to describe the dividing up of China among the imperialist powers of Great Britain, Japan, France, and others.

Folklore attests to a variety of unlikely melons that companies have distributed. American Molasses Company is said to have sent out barrels of molasses, American Distilling once paid shareholders with barrels of rye whiskey, and another liquor company produced bottles of bourbon labeled "Old Dividend" for its stockholders.

In the early part of this century, Wall Street used the ethnic slur **Irish dividend** to mean an assessment, when a company called upon stockbrokers to pay money rather than receive it. One letter in the humorous book *P.S. What Do You Think of the Market?*, written in 1919 by the pseudonymous A. Kustomer, has a customer complaining to his broker,

I aint criticizing you personally Eddie, y'understand, but I aint
exactly laughing all over since you make for me nothing but
Irish dividends.[10]

BONDS: BABIES, WAR BRIDES,
AND PLAIN VANILLA

"Gentlemen prefer bonds," Wall Streeters quipped in the late
1920s, parodying the 1925 book title *Gentlemen Prefer Blondes*
and expressing the appeal to conservative investors of bonds, which
have historically been safer than stocks. In various periods the
reputation of bonds has fallen and bond salesmen have suffered
from an image far from gentlemanly, as this joke shows:

> So there's this young guy that's become a bond salesman in
> New York, and he sees an old high school friend from upstate.
> They catch up on old times, tell what each is doing now. As
> they part, the salesman says, "Now whatever you do, if you see
> my folks, don't tell them I'm selling bonds. They think I'm
> playing piano in a whorehouse."

The tainted image came from the practice of selling questionable bonds at huge markups and milking the buyers dry. These
gullible customers longed to become *coupon clippers,* a term from
1882 that means people who live on the interest from their bonds.
The term, which evolved simply to mean wealthy people with
private incomes, came from the fact that bonds had detachable
coupons that owners presented for payment, one for each six
months of the bond's life. Today coupons are disappearing from
the financial scene, replaced by automatic payments.

In choosing bonds, conservative investors look for the *gilt-edged*
variety, a reliable, high-grade bond that produces steady interest.
Gilt-edged once applied to all good securities but has been replaced by *blue chip* when referring to stocks. The expression,
which has come to mean "first class" in general slang, may take

its name from the gilt edging on expensive notepaper, or the gold leaf on the edges of a book's pages.

In the 1920s, brokers used **gilt-edged** loosely to promote securities that proved to be anything but golden. Instead, many of the bonds were **junk,** which at that time referred to any worthless securities, cheap or expensive. Some buyers feel more comfortable paying high prices no matter the quality of the bond. According to the Wall Street adage, "It's easier to peddle high-class junk than low-class junk." **Junk** had several changes of meaning, and it came to mean specifically bonds with quality ratings of BB or lower. Until recently, **junk bonds** were issued solely by companies whose bonds once had high ratings that declined because of company problems. Such junk bonds form a **junk heap** that bargain hunters search through for low-priced junk that might rise again to glory against all odds.

In the 1970s, the investment bank of Drexel Burnham Lambert began to float junk bonds from emerging companies believed to be on their way up. Although these bonds have not fallen from a high rating, they are called **junk** because they are not yet of investment quality. These instruments have become the weapons of takeover artists in financing hostile takeovers, a controversial strategy.

Slang for bonds also draws on the nursery, the garden, and the kitchen. The macho trading world coyly terms a bond with a face value of $500 or less—some use it to mean $100 or less—that usually sells at a discount, a **baby bond.** The other **baby** in the market is the **war baby,** which is also slang for a child born when its father is away at war. **War babies** and **war brides** are stocks or bonds whose worth increases during war, such as the securities of companies that make weapons or steel; during the First World War a rally in these stocks brought about the **war bride boom of 1915.** A similar, popular term during the Second World War was **silver bullets,** government bonds and other securities that contributed to the war effort.

Flower bonds—flowers for short—take their name from the

flowers at a funeral or graveside, and are typically purchased by lawyers for investors on their deathbeds. These U.S. Treasury bonds are bought at a discount and cashed in at face value to pay the deceased bondholder's estate taxes.

Using another domestic metaphor, underwriters may spice up a bond issue with a *sweetener,* an extra feature designed to attract investors. Wall Street also calls these extras (which may be warrants, call options, or convertibility provisions) *kickers* and *bells and whistles* because they are meant to attract attention like the clamor of bells. When the bond contains no sweetening, brokers disparage it as *plain vanilla*—an unadorned, conventional offering. Even lower on the bond scale of taste is the *sour bond,* one of no worth.

FUTURES, OPTIONS, AND PIN-STRIPED PORK BELLIES

"There's an old joke about how to make a small fortune in the futures market . . . Start with a large fortune." Trading *futures contracts*—a term dating from 1870—is, as the joke implies, the riskiest business in the market. Because the margin requirements are low, from five to ten percent of the total price, a speculator can quickly lose an entire fortune.

In the hottest new addition to futures trading, investors speculate on the movement of the whole market, rather than just one stock, through stock market index futures in which the investor contracts to buy a "mythical basket of stocks" at a future date. For example, in buying the contract nicknamed *Spook,* the investor predicts how stocks tracked by the Standard & Poor's 100 index will do. For the person who wants to concentrate on one segment of the market, Wall Street offers *boutique indexes* that sum up the performance of a specialty such as computer, transportation, or utility stocks.

Whereas other futures contracts can result in delivery of a commodity in the form of a boxcar full of pork bellies or wheat, Spook and its counterparts have no physical item for delivery. No stock changes hands. Critics denounce the new practice as no better than outright gambling on which way the market will go. And indeed, before the U.S. exchanges offered stock market index futures, the London bookmaking concern of Ladbrokes was taking bets on the Dow Jones Industrial Average. It still makes book on the Dow, only now it buys U.S. index futures to hedge its bets.

No sooner had stock market index futures appeared than traders in Chicago dubbed them *pin-striped pork bellies,* because they combine the stock market—pin-striped suits—and the commodities market—pork belly contracts. The *pork bellies in pinstripes* opened at the Chicago Mercantile Exchange next to the pork belly pit, the wildest spot on the floor, and soon rivaled it in noise and excitement.

The abstract nature of stock market index futures, which lack any physical commodity, has led Wall Streeters to call trading in it a *shadow market,* a name they also apply to the newly organized market in options. Both markets are derivative, taking their life from the actual stock market. The market in options on listed stocks opened at the Chicago Board of Trade in 1973, although the over-the-counter market has offered options on stocks for years. In 1975, the Amex (American Stock Exchange) also added options, and other exchanges followed suit. At first only *calls* could be traded, but in 1977 *puts* became available as well.

A put is the right to sell, and a call is the right to buy, a fixed amount of stock at a set price within a limited period of time. The set price at which the option is written is the *striking price* or *strike price.* The metaphor behind *strike* hints at violence, but in fact most of the slang for options and commodities comes across as sexual. For example, when an investor buys a stock and the same day hedges it by purchasing a put, brokers call it a *married put.* If a writer owns the stock when writing a call option, they say he is *covered,* but if he does not own it, he is *naked* so that one trader might say to another, "I see you're naked on this one." Since being naked is risky business, brokerage houses require *naked option writers* to deposit money when trading options. According to one market observer, hints of sexuality are kept from the customer. "No broker in his right mind would talk to a conservative investor about naked options. . . . Such a dirty word as naked is never used." [11]

Options have given rise to numerous trading strategies whose names have at least faint sexual overtones, among them *strips, straps, straddles,* and *spreads.* Another entry in this list, the *strangle,* conveys a more violent image than the others. A strip combines two puts and a call, all with the same strike price and expiration date, while a strap has two calls and one put, with the same price and date. A strangle involves a long call and a long put on the same underlying security, with both options *out-of-the-money,* meaning above the security's price in the case of a call and below it in the case of a put.

Straddle, which has been part of the market lexicon since 1870, has several meanings. In options, it combines an equal number of puts and calls on the same stock with the same price and expiration date. In the commodities market, a straddle is the simultaneous purchase and sale of the same commodity in two different markets, or the purchase of a commodity future with an expiration date in one month and the sale of one with expiration in another month. An investor *straddles the market* when she is long of one stock and short of another, a means of hedging in an uncertain market.

Spreads resemble straddles. A spread in options combines a put and call with the same expiration dates but different striking prices, a strategy promoted by an 1875 writer:

> We recommend buying a Spread. Having a Put and Call on one contract, you are prepared to take advantage of the market whichever way it may go. If it advances so as to make a good profit you can Call the stock. Should it decline you can Put it. It is a matter of indifference to you whether it goes up or down. A person may be entirely unacquainted with stocks and be living thousands of miles away and yet know that he has two chances to win and only one to lose. [12]

At that time, spreads in stock options were also known as **spread-eagles.**

In commodities, a spread consists of being long of one contract and short of another of the same commodity but in different months, or the purchase and sale of the same commodity on different exchanges or with different delivery dates. The imagery used to describe spreads is unusually vivid, perhaps due to the abstract nature of the activity. Although superficially it appears that the commodities market deals with physical commodities, a joke that traders tell shows how false this notion is:

> Abe and Harry had been trading canned sardines for years on the Sardine Exchange. One day Abe happened to open a can of sardines that Harry had sold him. "How can you do this to me!" he yelled at his friend. "I'm ruined—these sardines are rotten." "Calm down, Abe," said Harry. "Don't you see? These aren't eating sardines—these are *trading* sardines."

In fact, most traders never take delivery on their contracts and would not have a can of sardines on the floor—if there were a Sardine Exchange.

The slang's dominant metaphor in options and commodities trading conveys a picture of a trader standing with his legs spread apart and the market lying between his two feet. The phrase **straddling the market** brings this image to mind as does describing the two sides of a spread as its **legs.** When an investor disposes of one side of the position, traders call it **lifting a leg, taking off a leg,** or **legging** the position. Market orders such as **touch but don't penetrate** and **participate but don't initiate** further the sexual imagery.

In concocting slang for a variety of spreads, traders once more prove their talent for wordplay, coming up with serious and humorous names. Starting with the mundane, a **bull spread** occurs when the trader is long the contract with the nearby date and short the later one, whereas the reversed situation regarding dates constitutes a **bear spread.** A whimsically named variation, the *butterfly spread,* said to have been pioneered by options expert Richard Handelsman, occurs in options and commodities. In options, the trader sells two calls, then buys two calls with one strike price above that of the calls sold and one below it, thus hedging from two directions. The commodities version consists of three legs where the outer two legs make up the *wings* of the butterfly. The middle leg has two contracts, and altogether the spread has an equal number of long and short positions.

In options the *sandwich spread,* with its structure straight from the deli, comprises four or more calls at three different striking prices: the two outer legs are long and the two sandwiched between them are short. Using another image from the world of food (or sex), a *jellyroll spread* combines long and short positions of puts and calls that have different expiration dates. In the energy futures pits, one finds the *crack spread,* which involves the margin between prices of refined products and crude oil.

A recent arrival on the scene, the *MOB spread,* where MOB stands for "munis over bonds," is based on the price differential between muni futures and Treasury bond futures. Traders created and christened it in 1985 when the Chicago Board of Trade introduced an index future on municipal bonds *(munis),* a basket of forty tax-exempt bonds that change almost weekly, traded immediately next to the pit for Treasury bond futures. A spread with a similar name, the *NOB spread,* stands for notes, meaning Treasury notes, over bonds.

Playing the spreads challenges even the most experienced trader and proves fatal for most amateurs. In a column in *The New York Times,* James Sterngold comments about one spread, "The MOB, a sophisticated trading technique generally used only by professionals, is akin to betting not on which horse will win a race, but by how much one horse will finish ahead of another."[13] In joking recognition of how dangerous spreads can be, traders and brokers have come up with a string of facetious nicknames for spreads: *Acapulco, alligator, cemetery,* and *O'Hare.* In the same humorous vein someone concocted the *Costa Rica hedge.*

The first two affect only outsiders, who must trade through a broker and therefore pay commissions. Whether the investor wins or loses, even the simplest spread produces four commissions, two to open plus two to close, adding up to an Acapulco spread that sends the broker to sunny Mexico for the weekend. Worse still, in an alligator spread, the client has no chance of profit. The broker's commissions amount to more money than the customer could possibly make, eating up potential profit the way an alligator devours a victim. A cemetery spread can hit an amateur or a professional at any time in any market: prices go the wrong way and instead of making a killing, the poor sucker gets "killed."

As a result of a cemetery spread, reckless professional traders may find themselves executing the O'Hare spread or its variant, the Costa Rica hedge. The trader takes an enormous risk, placing all his hopes on one transaction. If it doesn't come through, he resorts to the Costa Rica hedge, hightailing it for the balmy climate of Costa Rica and never coming back. Or the defeated trader may make a dash from LaSalle Street to the O'Hare airport, where he gives up the market to execute an O'Hare Spread: Sell Chicago, buy Mexico.

2

Mad Dog, Kitty Cat, and Marilyn Monroe: Nicknames for Stocks and Bonds

In 1983, when the Washington Public Power Supply System defaulted on bond payments, this joke immediately made the rounds on Wall Street, using a humorous-sounding nickname for the bond:

> An old man, a man 94 years old, goes to a doctor, who diagnoses the old man as having herpes. "Doc, it can't be true! I'm 94 years old. What will my wife say?" But the doctor assures him it is true. So the old man leaves, completely depressed, and sits outside on a park bench. A middle-aged man walks by and sees him. "What's the matter, Pop?" he asks. "What's the matter? I'm 94 years old, and I've got herpes. Herpes at 94!" "That's not so bad," the younger man replies. "Look at me. I'm 40, and I've got Whoopies at par!"

Whoopies, or *Whoops* as they are more commonly called, arose as a nickname out of the abbreviation for the power company, WPPSS. Nicknames for bonds and stocks pervade talk in Wall

Street today as they have for more than a hundred years. Traders off the exchange floors pepper their telephone conversations with them, while at the Exchange, traders and brokers ask specialists questions such as "How's your *Chocolate?*" for the price of Hershey stock, or the more risqué "How's your *Organ?*" to find out about Wurlitzer.

Traders christen the stocks with whimsical, sensible, and even obscene nicknames, drawing from the ticker symbol for the stock, its corporate name, or one of the corporation's products or services. In bond trading, the nicknames are based on similar sources. Occasionally, for both stocks and bonds, a nickname's origin has a more complex explanation. In the days when ITT stock was dubbed *Clara Bow,* the nickname made sense only if the listener knew that silent film actress Clara Bow had been known as "the It girl"—and that the ticker symbol for ITT was IT.

MOB, RAM, AND OKEFENOKEE

The symbols that appear on the ticker tape—once paper, now electronic—inspire many of the stock nicknames. For stocks listed on an exchange, the exchange in conjunction with the corporation assigns a one- to three-letter symbol, after determining that the symbol isn't in use elsewhere or reserved for use by another exchange. Although it's impossible to pin down the exact process whereby a nickname arises, probably when the stock starts to be traded and its symbol begins to be used, a trader looks at the letters in the symbol and turns them into one or more words. If the result proves catchy or useful enough, the nickname sticks.

Certain ticker symbols already spell a short word that becomes the nickname, such as Ramada Inn's symbol RAM, which remains *Ram.* But traders like to elaborate even on these ready-made names; for example, the nickname *Mob* for Mobil Oil comes straight from the symbol MOB, but, for fun, they sometimes extend it to *Mob Scene.* Caterpillar Tractor's nickname *Cat,* from CAT, occasionally gets expanded to *Kitty Cat.* Whoever christened *Pie-in-the-Sky* started with the ticker symbol, PIE, for

Piedmont Aviation, and played with it, and in a similar waggish spirit, traders in the past looked at the symbol for United Airlines (which now has a new name) and read it with a Southern accent, so that UAL became *You All.*

The nicknames *Ghost, Hummer,* and *Pacman*—from the video game of that name—are created by extending the ticker symbol into a longer word, derived from GHO for General Homes, HUM for Humana, and PAC for Pacific Telesis Group. By this principle, International Mineral & Chemicals, IGL, turns into *Igloo* and Oak Industries, with its symbol OAK, into *Okefenokee.*

By adding vowel sounds to symbols, traders come up with *Gorilla* for General Instrument (symbol GRL), *Missile* for Mercury Savings & Loan (MSL), *Spud* for Standard Products (SPD), and *Herbie* for H&R Block. *Gwiffy* for Great Western Savings (GWF), *Teddy* for Teledyne (TDY), and *Dump* for Dome Petroleum (DMP) work the same way, as did *Nitwit* for Northwest Industries (NWT), now Farley Northwest.

The nickname *Murder* comes from stretching out the symbol MDR for McDermott; when McDermott stock falls, the traders get a kick from observing that "Murder got killed." On the Amex floor in the 1970s, Kleinert's was dubbed *Killer,* from its symbol KLR, and Devon Apparel, DEV, was *Devil,* prompting the same kind of comment: "Killer got killed" and "The Devil got murdered."

In other nicknames, the letters in the ticker symbol become the initial letters in entire words. For example, the PWJ for the Paine Webber Group becomes *Peanut Butter With Jelly* and the DH for Dayton Hudson becomes *Dead Head,* perhaps from the old railroad slang of D.H. for Dead Head, used to describe non-paying passengers. RB, the symbol for Redding Bates, translates into *Roast Beef;* the first two letters in LLX, the symbol for Louisiana Land, turn into *Lousy Louie;* and, in times past, the YB for Youngstown Steel became *Yellowbellies,* a general slang word for cowards.

The MM for Marine Midland Banks sparked the slang names *Minnie Mouse* as well as *Mickey Mouse,* a nickname also used for Disney stock. Punsters on the floor sometimes take the ticker symbol MMM for Minnesota Mining & Manufacturing (often known as 3M) and combine it with the Mickey Mouse from MM to make *Mickey Mouse's Mother.* In other wordplay, traders take one slang name and twist it into yet another slang name for the same company; thus, *United Jewish Bank,* slang for United Jersey Bank (UJB), becomes *United Bagel Bank.*

Utility customers of Pacific Gas & Electric who hope to disrupt the company a little make out their checks to *Pigs, Goats & Elephants,* from PG&E, the company's widely used abbreviation that is also its ticker symbol. Traders at the Pacific Stock Exchange have sometimes adopted this nickname, but more often call the stock *Gas* or *Peggy.*

INITIALS AND INITIATIONS

"I knew, of course, there must be a limit to the advances and an end to the crazy buying of A.O.T.—Any Old Thing," said a character in a 1923 novel, using a then common Wall Street witticism that played on stock nicknames. Around the same time, the book *P.S. What Do You Think of the Market?* by A. Kustomer, parodied the nicknames that come from abbreviations. Writing about Baldwin G.T.C., the author commented,

> I always thought it meant Guaranty Trust Company, but a friend of mine says they aint in the brokerage business, and that it means Gamblers Take Chances.[1]

In the stock market, the market order GTC stands for Good Till Canceled.

The fictional social critic Mr. Dooley also had fun with stock abbreviations a few decades earlier, talking in his Irish brogue about an acquaintance who had bought a "large block iv D.O.P.&E." and commenting on "shares of S.N.A.&P., which pay on'y six per cint."[2]

Wall Street folklore has another group of imaginary stocks with imaginary ticker symbols, which previously played a role in initiating new stock traders. Older members at the NYSE and Pacific Stock Exchange remember the days when a novice would receive a big order for one of these hypothetical stocks, little realizing it didn't exist. *Coney Island Sand,* with the symbol CIS, *Douglas Fir, Hawaiian Pineapple, Trans-Atlantic Bridge, Third Avenue Railroad, Ohio Packing*—these were some of the gag stocks.

The new trader would be directed to where, say, Coney Island Sand allegedly traded, and find the post surrounded by a crowd of traders who were in on the joke. Before the newcomer could get in his order, the price started rising dramatically—and he just couldn't catch the specialist's attention. Up, up, the stock would go, maybe twenty points, with ten minutes of agony before he could get in his bid. But then as he was turning away, after having filled the order at a high price, the price would start to plummet, leading him to believe he had seriously botched up his first big transaction. Those who recall the trick say that sometimes the novice's face would turn so white that his tormentors would cut the trick short to spare him more pain.

PLAYING WITH CORPORATE NAMES AND PRODUCTS

The nicknames *Dog* or *Speedy Dog* for Greyhound Corporation, *Georgia Peach* for Georgia Pacific, and *Okie Gas* for Oklahoma Gas illustrate the other common way, besides using ticker symbols, that traders create stock nicknames, that is, by playing with the corporate name. Using this method, a trader who wants to buy Chesebrough-Pond's asks for *Cheeseburgers* and one who wants Lucky Stores asks for *Unlucky.*

Burlington Northern shortens into *Burlie* (although it's also known as *Beanie* from its symbol BNI), Honeywell into *Honey,* Navistar into *Navy,* SmithKline Beckman into *Smitty,* Zweig Fund into *Zwiggy,* and Kimberley into *Kimbies.* In some cases, the front end drops off the corporate title, making *Zoil* for Pennzoil and *Roid* for Polaroid. In other cases, the nickname comes from the middle, such as *Semi* for National Semiconductor and *Busty* for Combustion Engineering.

Companies with Petroleum in their titles inevitably have it changed to Pete in the nickname, so that over the years, *Mexican Pete, Pete Products, Pontiac Pete,* and *Occidental Pete* or *Oxy Pete* have been part of the lexicon.

Traders call a good many stocks by obvious shortened names: *Air* for British Air, *Express* for American Express, *Telephone* for AT&T, *Soup* for Campbell Soup, *Decker* for Black & Decker. A few corporations that are household words have long been known in the market by simple nicknames: *Radio* for RCA, *Motors* for General Motors, *Steel* for U.S. Steel, *Tire* for Goodyear, *Mills* for General Mills.

Corn Flakes, Dog Chow, Gum, and *Whiskey*—these nicknames arose because Wall Streeters associated a certain product with a corporation and, given the corporate names Kellogg's, Ralston, Wrigley, and Seagram's, most Americans could probably match them up with the stock nicknames. Along the same lines, Milton Bradley, no longer traded, took its nickname *Toys* from the games it marketed, and Weyerhauser takes its from the company's main product, *Timber.* The familiar F.W. Woolworth is called just what many shoppers call it, the *Five & Ten.*

Traders have had a field day nicknaming Community Psychiatric Centers with the uncomplimentary results of *Loony Tunes, Funny Farms, Crazy House* and—in conjunction with its symbol CMY—*Crazy Mary.* Equally disrespectful nicknames emerged for National Cash Register Company in the 1950s, drawing on ethnic stereotypes to come up with *Scotch Piano* and *Jewish Piano.*

BO DEREKS AND JAMES BONDS

The Wall Street wits who nickname bonds and other debt securities, like their stock market counterparts, rely on abbreviations, and on organization names, products, services, or activities. Straight from the abbreviations, bonds of Northern Indiana Public becomes *Nips,* while, by filling out abbreviations with extra sounds, traders dub bonds for Southern California Public Power Authority, *Scappas,* for Los Angeles Department of Water/Power, *Dewaps,* and for Lower Colorado River Authority, *Locos.* The question, "Do you want some *Martas?*" refers to bonds for Metropolitan Atlanta Rapid Transit Authority, whose initials also translate into the derogatory quip "Moving Africans Rapidly Through Atlanta."

Sacramento Municipal Utility District bonds have the unattractive nickname, *Sacmuds,* while Tacoma Light and Power and Seattle Light and Power have the more appealing *Taclights* and *Sealights.* Traders dub Washington Suburban Sanitary District, *Washtubs,* Missouri Power & Light, *Miseries,* and Washington D.C. Public Housing Authority, *Alley Cats.*

Placing an order for *Big Macs* on Wall Street results not in hamburgers from McDonald's fast food chain, but in bonds of the Municipal Assistance Corporation, created in 1975 to alleviate New York City's financial crisis. The bond, which is widely known outside financial circles, gets its nickname from the Big in "Big Apple" plus the corporation's initials.

The general public is also acquainted with a virtual family of debt securities: *Fannie Mae* (FNMA), Federal National Mortgage Association; *Ginnie Mae* (GNMA), Government National Mortgage Association; *Sallie Mae* (SLMA), Student Loan Marketing Association; *Nellie Mae,* New England Educational Loan Marketing Corporation; and brother *Freddie Mac,* Federal Home Loan Mortgage Corporation. Sounding like another member of the clan, *Sammie Bee* stands for Small Business Administration guaranteed loans securities.

Bonds, which expire in certain years, sometimes take their nicknames from an association with that year's numerals. For example, when the U.S. Treasury issued bonds due to expire in 1990, the Street dubbed them *Gay Nineties,* from the nickname for the 1890s. Traders enjoy the term for U.S. Treasury bonds that expire in the year 2007, *James Bonds,* based, as moviegoers know, on the code name Agent 007 for fictional spy James Bond. Also from the movies, quipsters termed U.S. Treasury bonds that mature in the year 2010 *Bo Dereks,* after the shapely star of the movie *10;* hence the telephone conversations in which one trader asks another, "Do you want some Bo Dereks?"

Other numbers can prompt bond nicknames. In the 1950s, the market offered **two brothers,** two issues of 2 percent bonds, and **three little sisters,** three issues of 2 percent bonds. During the next decade, everyone wanted **magic fives,** U.S. bonds issued at 5 percent, while also on the scene were **discos** or **Whiskey Diskies,** bonds always selling at a discount.

Zeros or **zippers** in today's Wall Street lingo mean zero-coupon bonds, a form of investment introduced in 1982. Issued at less than face value, they mature in more than a year, produce no income while held, and are redeemed at face value. Traders dub zeros issued in serial form **zerials.**

Brokerage houses started marketing a host of zero-coupon bonds and christening them with cute acronyms, arrived at through long, convoluted underlying names. First came CATS, LIONs, and TIGRs: Certificates of Accrual on Treasury Securities, Lehman Investment Opportunity Notes, and Treasury Investment Growth Receipts. Then, with equally dry official names, came STARS, DARTS, MAPS, AMPS, and CAMPS.

The naming trend escalated into longer acronyms and more complex underlying names, from FASTBACs, First Automotive Short-term Bonds and Certificates, to that unlikely animal, OPOSSMS, Options to Purchase or Sell Specific Mortgage-backed Securities. Not all issue abbreviations are planned, as a *Wall Street Journal* article of February 18, 1987, reports.

> The uncontrived names of some securities actually form acronyms, but these rarely make useful marketing tools. First Boston, for instance, once underwrote an offering of secured-lease obligation bonds. It used the full name.

ELSIE, SPUTNIK, AND CAPTAIN MARVEL

To those who have never read Captain Marvel comics, the nickname **Shazam** for CalMat Co. presents a mystery. The comic fan who bestowed it, though, looked at the ticker symbol CZM and saw letters that combined Captain Marvel and a favorite exclamation from the comic, "Shazam." An even more indirect connection inspired the nickname during the 1960s of *Say Hey* for J.W. Mays, Inc. Although baseball player Willie Mays had no business connection with the Mays department store chain, his pet phrase "Say Hey!" gave the stock its nickname.

As Say Hey and Shazam illustrate, the choice of a nickname may have a story behind it. When traders called Borden stock *Elsie*—or sometimes *Moo Moo*—and Waldorf System *Red Apple,* they were thinking of the cow named Elsie pictured on Borden's dairy products and the Red Apple logo for Waldorf's restaurant chain. In the 1960s, the nickname *Crosby* for Minute Maid referred to Bing Crosby's role in advertising the orange juice.

The story behind Standard Packaging's stock nickname hinges on when it was listed: November 17, 1957. A few weeks earlier, Russia had stunned the world by sending the satellite known as Sputnik into orbit. So, even though Standard Packaging had nothing to do with outer space, when its stock was launched at the NYSE, its assigned symbol SPK immediately sparked the nickname *Sputnik.*

Sometimes only a floor trader or an old-timer can explain a name's origin. For example, when Jamaica Water & Power was listed at the NYSE, it received the symbol JWP, and was traded on the floor in the same vicinity as the stock of King World, with its similar symbol of KWP. Its nickname, *Jew World,* obviously takes "Jew" from the JW, and less obvious to outsiders—"World" from King World.

Longtime traders know when a nickname comes from a previous corporate name or stock symbol. When U.S. Rubber changed its name to Uniroyal, Wall Street kept its old tag, **Rubber.** And for years after American Radiator & Sanitation Service changed its symbol DT to AST, traders still wanted to know, "How's your *Jitters?*" The general slang D.T.'s for delirium tremens provided an irresistible nickname that outlasted the ticker symbol it came from.

LONDON'S CORAS AND DORAS

The habit of nicknaming securities seems to have started, not on Wall Street, but at the London Exchange, judging from the large number of nicknames recorded in the nineteenth century. In 1895, writer A. J. Wilson listed more than eighty "Slang, or Corrupted Names," as he called them, warning ordinary investors to avoid the slang.[3] Another British writer in 1901 offered explanations for some of the terms' origins, which might otherwise be difficult to determine.[4] Most of the early nicknames stood for British or American Railroads stocks, such as *Berthas* for London, Brighton & South Coast Railway; *Clara, Clarette, Cora,* and *Flora* for three types of Caledonian Railway stocks; *Nora* for a Great Northern issue, and *Sara* for one from Manchester, Sheffield & Lincolnshire. The Great North of Scotland Railway was known as *Haddocks,* while Buenos Ayres & Great Southern Railway was *Bags,* derived from its initials.

Among American railroads—known as a whole as *Yankee Rails* or *Yankees*—Wabash Preferred Shares became *Boshs,* Denver & Rio Grande Preference Shares *Damps,* and New York, Lake Erie, & Western Second Mortgage Bonds *Snipes.* New York, Pennsylvania & Ohio First Mortgage Bonds went by the uncomplimentary *Apes.*

Securities other than railroads prompted more varied names. The London traders adopted *Marbles* for Marbella Iron Ore Shares, *Beefs* for Eastmans Ordinary, and *Bones* for Wickens, Pease, & Co. They dubbed Aerated Bread Shares *Breads* and, in the spirit of whimsy, called fractions of the shares *Bread Crumbs. Knackers* served as the nickname for Harrison, Barber & Company, the chief London horse slaughterers, from the slang word "knackers" for worn-out horses. Stock for Samuel Allsopp & Sons, a brewery, was nicknamed *Ales* or *Slops,* while stock of Arthur Guinness, Sons & Co., which produced ale, was *Stout,* from a type of ale.

Because the Eastern Extension Telegraph Company lines extended to China, its shares became *Chinas.* Fractions of the shares of Salmon & Gluckstein, a large tobacconist, were *Fags,* a slang term for cigarettes. Traders called shares of the British Cotton and Wool Dyers' Association *Slubbers,* from a term for textile workers. Two Per Cent Virginia Funded Debt Bonds became, inevitably, *Virgins,* while certain war bonds took their name from military uniforms, *Khakis.*

The area at the London Exchange where deals were made in South African companies and mines was known as the *Kaffir Circus,* with its stock called *Kaffirs,* the name of a southern African people, and trades in West African Gold and Exploration Shares took place in the *Jungle Market,* another area of the exchange. Shares in Australian concerns were dubbed *Kangaroos,* though the writer doesn't indicate if their prices jumped around.

Thirty years later, according to A. S. J. Osborn's *The Stock Exchange,* London traders still used Bags, Breads, Slubbers, Yankees, and Kaffirs as stock names. Fags had been shifted to another stock, drawn from that company's name of Antofagasta & Bolivia Railway.

Other nicknames on Osborn's list included *Friscos* for San Francisco Mines, *Imps* for Imperial Tobacco Company, *Bats* for British American Tobacco, and *Rags* for Goldfield Rhodesian Development. Londoners shared two 1930 nicknames for railroads with American traders: *Canpacs* for Canadian Pacific and *Milks* for Chicago, Milwaukee & St. Paul, which also went by *Paul* and *St. Paul* in the U.S.

FROM HARLOTS TO BUGS

Wall Streeters also began coining names for the stocks and bonds in the nineteenth century. As early as 1873, they dubbed Michigan Southern & Northern Indiana Railroad *Old Southern,* or *Old Sow* for short, and Prairie de Chien Railroad *Prairie Dog.*

In the late 1800s, market giant Daniel Drew, known as *Uncle Daniel,* manipulated the stock of Erie Railroad so often that he ruined its reputation as a legitimate investment. Erie's nicknames reflected the damage, comparing the stock to a woman of ill-repute: the **Harlot of the Rails** and the **Scarlet Woman of Wall Street.** His contemporaries joked about Drew's blatant control over Erie stock, saying,

> Uncle Daniel says up—Erie goes up.
> Uncle Daniel says down—Erie goes down.
> Uncle Daniel says wiggle-waggle, and it bobs both ways.

Pan Handle, P-Mail, and **Trolley,** which were listed in 1900 in S. A. Nelson's *The ABCs of Wall Street,* stood for Pittsburgh, Cincinnati, Chicago, & St. Louis; Pacific Mail; and Brooklyn Rapid Transit. People's Gas took its nickname from its ticker symbol, P.O., **Post Office,** while railroads owned by Jay Gould were grouped together as **Goulds** and those owned by the Vanderbilt family as **Vanderbilts.**

Some of the slang nicknames from 1900 and earlier survived in Wall Street for decades. Nelson mentioned **Mops** for Missouri Pacific; **Nipper** for Northern Pacific; **Katie** for Missouri, Kansas & Texas; **Big Four** for Cleveland, Cincinnati, Chicago & St. Louis; and **Atch** for Atchison, Topeka & Sante Fe. These railroad stock nicknames were still in use in 1960, according to an article published that year by Clayton S. Scott.

About such old nicknames, Scott observes that it is impossible to know if they originated in the financial community or were borrowed from general usage. He cites as the most famous corporate nickname **Nickel Plate Road,** for New York, Chicago, & St. Louis Railroad, and he explains the slang name's origin:

> Built in competition with Vanderbilt's New York Central, it was offered for sale to him at such an exorbitant price that, according to legend, Vanderbilt exclaimed that the rails must be made of nickel plate.[5]

Scott adds that the nickname bestowed by Vanderbilt stuck so well that in 1960 many brokers did not know the stock's real name.

A list with some amusing stock nicknames appeared in a 1916 publication titled A *Short Story of the Stock Exchange,* "Compliments of Robert Lossing Niles." It included *Coffee, Cakes & Ice Cream* for C.C. & I.C.; *Delay, Linger & Wait* for Delaware, Lackawanna & Western; *Never Did & Can't (Pay)* for Newburgh, Dutchess & Connecticut; and *Wash Lost Everything* for Wheeling & Lake. Another name listed, *Bug,* for Brooklyn Union Gas, is still part of Wall Street lingo.

Traders liked to pair nicknames, designating Big and Little. For Northern Pacific and Union Pacific stocks, the "big" meant preferred stock, the "little," common stock. Thus, *Big Nipper* and *Little Nipper* (sounding a lot like the constellation) and *Big Union* and *Little Union.* Niles records Cleveland, Lorain & Wheeling as *Connor's Little Wash,* and Chicago Great Western as *Connor's Big Wash,* but doesn't explain the joke.[6]

WHY NICKNAMES?

Traders past and present have sought humor, brevity, or clarity in the nicknames they create. Humor is indispensable in the high-tension world of Wall Street, and perhaps inevitable where so many spend so much time talking. A new, funny nickname, like a joke, starts a deal over the telephone on a congenial note, and adds a laugh to conversations on the exchange floors.

In the case of some nicknames, the humor depends on the corporation's product. For example, in the 1960s and 1970s, stock of Simmons Company, which made mattresses, became known as *America's Playground* or *World's Playground.* Wilson Pharmaceutical, producer of drugs, was dubbed *Goofball,* from the slang for tranquilizers, and traders extended the theme to two other Wilson companies spun off by LTV, also giving them names from balls: *Golfball* for Wilson Sporting and *Meatball* for its meatpacking corporation.

More often the ticker symbol inspires the wit. SRO, symbol for Southland Royalty, prompted the name *Standing Room Only,* while in the 1960s, HBA, symbol for H&B American, turned into *Hubba-Hubba,* a World War II come-on for picking up a pretty woman. Indulging in wordplay, traders called United Industrial Corporation **Peek-a-Boo,** from the symbol UIC ("You I See").

Although Standing Room Only has no fewer syllables than Southland Royalty, usually the slang name is shorter than the full corporate name, an important feature during busy trading. The faster a trader can holler a name, the more trades he can cram into a hectic day. In the pursuit of brevity, traders at the NYSE today change Louisiana General Service to **Legs** (symbol LGS), Storage Technology to **Stick** (STK), Leaseway Transportation to **Lettuce** (LTC), and Financial of Santa Barbara to **Frisbee** (FSB).

Municipal bonds especially demand trimming, since they take their unwieldy official names from government agencies and utility companies. Traders have whittled down Jacksonville Electric Authority to **Jax,** Municipal Electric Authority of Georgia to **Meags,** and Puerto Rico Industrial Development Corporation to **Pridcos.**

Even more than brevity, traders value clarity in nicknames, because misunderstandings can translate into financial losses. For example, in the 1960s, Texas Gulf Producing and Texas Gulf Sulphur could have invited confusion in busy trading because they shared their first two words, but having **Teddy Roosevelt** and **Tough Guy** (sometimes known as **Tough Gus**) as nicknames eliminated confusion. Similarly, on today's options floor at the Pacific Stock Exchange, McDonald's and McDonnell Douglas, which initially sound the same, will not be mixed-up, thanks to their unmistakable and unforgettable nicknames: **Murder Burgers** and **Mad Dog.**

Calling out these two nicknames also makes more sense than calling out their similar ticker symbols, McD and MD. Since the alphabet has only twenty-six letters and the world of trading has thousands of stocks, many symbols share letters and therefore sound alike. Listeners find it easier to distinguish nicknames from each other than one series of letters from another, and traders find it easier to recall catchy nicknames than dull abbreviations—a blessing to those who deal in dozens of stocks.

That some stocks share the same nickname seems, on the face of it, to defeat the aim of distinguishing between stocks. However, both Wall Street and the stock exchange floors are made up of little worlds with distinct boundaries. The Pacific Stock Exchange members could call Crocker National Bank (when it was listed) *Chicken,* while on the opposite coast, the NYSE used the same name for Church's Fried Chicken, with no harm done. In the municipal bond market, where *Chessies* are Chesapeake Bay Bridge & Tunnel Authority bonds, a trader won't confuse them with CSX stock, called *Chessie* at the NYSE and PSE.

Even within the walls of the NYSE floor, *Bessie* means either Bethlehem Steel (BS) or Boston Edison (BSE); but as long as they are traded at different posts, no one is confused. Although some floor brokers, especially the two-dollar ones, roam the entire exchange floor, for the most part the others stay in a limited territory. Whereas the roamers will know dozens of nicknames, those confined to one area will only know nicknames for stocks listed at the posts nearby.

Physical boundaries also explain why one stock can have more than one nickname. At any post where only one gasoline, telephone, or airline stock trades, a broker can say simply, "How's your gas?", "How's your telephone?", or "How's your air?" without causing confusion. They can ask, "How's Jenny?" at any post that lists just one of the corporations that start with "General."

On the two trading floors at the Pacific Stock Exchange in San Francisco, in separate but connected rooms, the rowdier options floor adopts some different nicknames than the more sedate equities side. They prefer *Murder Burgers* for McDonald's to the more widely used *Hamburgers,* and *Dick* for Digital Equipment (DEC), instead of *Deck.* While the equities floor traders enjoy calling McDonnell Douglas *Mother Duck,* their counterparts in options go with *Mad Dog.*

Sometimes a stock will have two or three nicknames, all of them used on the same exchange floor, all fairly easily recognized. The specialist in a stock will be conversant with the several names, although an individual broker may have heard of only one. At the NYSE, different members call Houston National Gas (HNG) *Hanger*—with a hard "g"—or *Hangnail.* Solant's ticker symbol SLT brought about two nicknames, neither of which would please the corporation: *Slit* and *Slut.* Champion International is the rhythmical *Cha-Cha* to some, from its symbol CHA, but *Champ* to others, from its name. And, for a stock no one can ignore, everyone on the floor recognizes that *Beamer, Eye-Beam,* and *Big Blue* all mean IBM.

History plays a role in duplicate nicknames—nicknames are recycled for different stocks over time, and other stocks find their nicknames changed. *Nipper* was famous as the name for Northern Pacific, but now serves as one of the nicknames for Northern Indiana Public Service. *Panhandle,* once Pittsburgh, Cincinnati, Chicago & St. Louis Railroad, today means Public Service of New Hampshire (PNH). Perhaps because traders love to ask for *Whiskey,* that nickname over the years has stood for West Kentucky Coal and Wisconsin Central, and now stands for Seagram's.

Ford Motors once wore the nicknames *Tin Lizzy* and *Flivver,* from slang for certain car models, but as knowledge of those terms faded, traders resorted to the simpler *Ford,* whose symbol is the single letter "F." Although ITT has been *Father Divine* as well as Clara Bow in its time, most traders now call it the straightforward *I-Phone.*

LOLAS, ZSA ZSA GABORS, AND OTHER WOMEN'S NAMES

Women, insults, and obscenities—in looking at the body of nicknames, past and present, these three categories stand out as sources for the slang names. Perhaps for the same reason that men name ships after women—ships that often have no female crew members—male traders have always named stocks after women. As mentioned above, nineteenth-century London traders bought and sold Berthas, Claras, Clarettes, Coras, Floras, Noras, and Saras. In the United States, too, traders see women's names in numerous ticker symbols. Besides Bessie, Katie, and Peggy, given earlier, the lexicon in recent years has included *Becky* for Beckmann

Instruments, *Amy* or *Old Mona* for American Medical International, *Maggie* for Magnavox, and *Pamela* for Pamida. Among the Jennies are *Jennie Tel* for General Telephone and *Jennie Electric* for General Electric.

WM for Western Maryland Railroad used to be *Wet Mary* or *Weeping Mary; Rebecca* indicated Republic Steel Corp.; *Old Women* was New York, Ontario & Western Railway; and *Hers* stood for Helena Rubinstein, Inc. Minneapolis Moline was *Minnie;* Electric & Musical Industries, EMI, *Emmy;* Allis Chambers, *Alice;* and Anaconda, *Annie.* Molybdenum Corporation, MLY, was *Molly,* and when Molybdenum of Canada was listed, with the letters MDT, traders quickly dubbed it *Midnight Molly.*

Bo Derek and Clara Bow are not the only famous females unknowingly to lend their names. In the 1960s, Italian Development Bonds were better known as *Lolas,* and Southern Bell Telephone securities, taking their name from that famous Southern belle, were *Scarlett O'Haras.* Continental Can at one time was called *Zsa Zsa Gabor.*

BELITTLING BARBS

Among corporate executives who have heard their company's nicknames, those whose stock has a woman's name should feel relieved, in view of other nicknames in use. Some besides the female nicknames evoke harmless images: *Mother's Oats* for Quaker Oats; *Music* for MCA (Music Corporation of America); *Fido* for Family Dollar Stores, from FDO; and *Uncle* for UNC, Inc. National Distillers could do worse than *Doctor,* from its symbol DR, and in an era when teenagers exclaim "Dynamite" for approbation, General Dynamics does well with *Dynamite.*

Certain nicknames even have an all-American ring, such as *Hockey,* adopted because Newhall Land Farming's symbol NHL also stands for National Hockey League; and *Football,* the nickname of American Family Insurance, from AFL, initials of the American Football League. Also from the football world, the ticker symbol FG gave U.S. Fidelity & Guarantee, no longer listed, the nickname *Field Goal.*

Some slang names may strike the company as even too cute, such as the now obsolete *Fuzzy Wuzzy* for Fairbanks Whitney, FW. Better cute than disparaging, though. Of the names mentioned earlier, *Dead Head, Unlucky, Lousy Louie, Goofball,* and, of course, *Murder Burgers* do not flatter the companies and their products—companies that spend large amounts on advertising. *House of Frogs* or *House of Fags* for House of Fabrics (HF) would hardly be the choice of management.

Along the same lines, *Slob* for Schlumberger (SLB), *Funny Bank* for First National Bank of Chicago (FNB), and *Big Nose Louie* for Beneficial Corporation (BNL) don't gibe with the public image corporations normally seek, while the nickname *Global Maroon* for Global Marine conjures up pictures of the company's customers stranded on desert islands, even though Global Marine's primary business is offshore oil and gas drilling. Innkeepers could only frown upon the previous nicknames for two motel chains, *Hot Beds* for Holiday Inn (HIA) and the unsavory *Roach* for Royal Inns of America (ROA), probably inspired by the cockroach remedy called the Roach Motel and certainly likely to put off customers.

In fact, the public rarely comes into contact with these nicknames, which are part of the private Wall Street lingo and largely confined to traders. Furthermore, in most cases, the traders are not passing judgment on a corporation or disparaging it in some personal way. The nicknames come from wordplay based on the corporate name or the ticker symbol. Wall Streeters who use the names sometimes know the symbol but can't identify the corporation, much less what business it is in.

THE UNPRINTABLES

With the virtual absence of women until recently on Wall Street and especially on the exchange floor, traders have felt free to use language they would avoid in a more formal—or female-inhabited—setting, coming up with nicknames that move from the merely disparaging into the obscene. To be fair, sometimes the ticker symbol practically spells out an off-color nickname. For example, it didn't take much imagination to derive **Pricks** from Par Pharmaceutical's PRX. Other names, however, couldn't have been predicted by those assigning the ticker symbol. The BA for Boeing does not automatically bring to mind **Bare Ass,** its nickname at the NYSE.

Unfortunately for the researcher, although obscene nicknames presumably thrived in the oral realm all along, they were not recorded in print until the 1970s, when books and magazine articles occasionally shared with readers a few racy nicknames. Even then, *Business Week* of July 29, 1972, left it up to the reader to fill in the blanks:

> What floor traders call Shaer Shoe (SHS) and Technical Tape (TTI) cannot be printed in *Business Week*. Perhaps the heaviest cross any company has to bear was what the Street called the old Fairbanks Morse stock, whose symbol before the company vanished into Colt Industries was FKM. Recently, FKM reappeared on the Amex tape, and word spread like lightning around the Street that "FKM is back." The new butt of it all: Fluke Mfg. Co.[7]

A look at more recent publications or a trip to any exchange floor will reveal that many companies today have equally vulgar nicknames. An outsider does not have to look far to see how certain names came about, based on the corporate name. Given a group of men with time on their hands—as traders have when the market is slow—is it surprising that they nicknamed Upjohn **Hard-On;** Hughes Tool **Huge Tool;** Snap-on Tool **Dildo;** and Hancock Fabrics **Cock**?

That the Street came up with **Ass** from Associated Spring's AAS or **Prick** from Product Research's PRC wins no prizes in creativity. **Eat Me** for Emerson Radio from the ticker symbol EME took no big stretch of the imagination. Traders have called Pacific Southwest Airlines, PSA, **Pisser**—or when its stock was particularly low, *Piece of Shit Airlines.* Public Service of Colorado, PSR, also sports the nickname *Pisser;* and Dorchester Gas, DGS, does no better with *Dogshit.* Not to be left out, bond traders have played with words to come up with the name for Massachusetts State Municipal Wholesale Electric, *Massholes.*

Of Portland General & Electric's two nicknames, from its symbol PGN, the milder *Pigeon* may be more intuitive, but is certainly less catchy than *Pig Nuts.* An outsider can explain away *Knockers* for Northrup (NOC) and *Pussy* for Pillsbury (PSY), but is left to wonder about the creator who came up with the nickname for First Wisconsin Bank, from the symbol FWB: *Fat Wally's Balls.*

GONE BUT NOT FORGOTTEN

Certain nicknames never die. Years after the stocks they stood for are no longer traded, these waggish names hold a secure place in stock market folklore. Thus, traders who know nothing about what the Air Reduction Company was like or how its stock traded, still smile about its nickname, *Shut the Door.* What Wall Streeter can forget that tribute to a movie star's figure, the nickname for the Welbilt Corporation—*Marilyn Monroe.* Or the jest that stuck as the nickname for the Pittsburgh Screw and Bolt Company? The inimitable *Love 'em and Leave 'em.*

3

Suckers, Scalpers, and the Smart Money Boys: People in the Market

THE PUBLIC IS ALWAYS WRONG

A Wall Street legend tells us that in 1929 Joseph P. Kennedy encountered a shoeshine boy who jubilantly predicted the market would keep going up. Then and there Kennedy decided to dump his stocks and start selling short, for the littlest of the little guys could only be wrong. When the market crashed and other investors were crushed, Kennedy emerged with a fortune.

The legend illustrates the popular Wall Street proverb, "The public is always wrong," in which *the public* refers to people who buy or sell small amounts of stock, allegedly always at the wrong time. They buy just as the market is about to fall and sell just before it goes up. Wall Streeters say that the public enters the market "when its greed grows stronger than its fear," by which time a rally has reached its peak and is on its way down.

The proverb and legend exaggerate the disdain that brokers as an occupational group feel toward their customers. Because brokers work on commission, they must please the customers no matter how rude or greedy they are. The exchanges and brokerage houses have spent large amounts of money wooing the public with campaigns to "Own Your Own Share of American Business," "Invest in America," and take part in "People's Capitalism," and the brokers must put on a facade as welcoming as the slogans. To relieve the tension that results from constant courtesy, brokers express a heightened hostility through the slang they share with their colleagues behind the public's back. Like many occupational groups, brokers use slang to create solidarity and to vent shared emotions not allowed on the job. By creating a specialized language as well as proverbs and legends, the group excludes and even mystifies the public.

Brokerages have found they can attract the public by making brokerage offices easily accessible. This encourages **walk-ins,** new, usually unsophisticated, customers who wander in to try their hand at the market. Firms install electronic ticker-tapes in their lobbies so investors can drop by to check the latest stock prices. Some spend hours watching the tape, no doubt unaware that the brokers have dubbed them **lobby rats** or **lobby lizards,** borrowed from lounge lizard, general slang for an idler.

Of course, many members of the public regard themselves as canny investors and assume that others constitute the so-called public. Hence the widely known "Bigger Fool Theory" or "Other Idiot Principle," which contends that you can buy a stock at a ridiculously high price, knowing some other idiot will pay you even more for it. The principle doesn't always hold good, as an old joke shows:

> A fellow's broker sold him thousands of shares of a penny-mining stock, and called him each hour to sell him more. It started at fifteen cents, and each hour the price went up. By the afternoon the investor owned 20,000 shares. His broker calls at 2:30. "Your stock is up to $1.50," he says. "Great," says the customer, "sell it." The broker pauses, then asks, "To who?"

The member of the public who does not buy or sell much is frequently called the **little guy,** the **little man,** the **little fellow,** or, collectively, the **little people.** Another market term for investors who dabble in stocks is *outsiders,* recorded as early as 1848 to mean those other than professional or regular investors. These outsiders make up the *odd-lot public* or *odd lotters,* terms of some contempt; to buy an *odd lot* (known in Canada as a *broken lot*) is to buy fewer than one hundred shares (a *round lot*) of a stock at a time. Professionals view an increase in odd-lot purchases, indicating more amateurs in the market, as a signal to sell, once more implying that the public is wrong.

They say that the odd-lotter has *weak hands,* one of the images of weakness that occur in market slang, where the stock market itself can be weak or strong as can the market in an individual stock. *Weak hands* characterize those investors who hold securities that they would sell for a slight profit, in which case the stocks are *weakly held.* In contrast, the term *strong hands,* which dates back to the 1920s, applies to investors who tend to hold securities for long periods of time. *Weak sisters* buy a stock purportedly as an investment, to be held six months or more, but sell it to take a profit as soon as the price rises; or they may claim to have faith in a stock they own, yet sell it if the price falls. Generally, Wall Street calls any person or organization that is not holding its own a weak sister.

In recent years, however, many a small investor has indirectly gained power and influence in the market by becoming part of a large investor, a mutual fund. *The Wall Street Journal* reported in February 1986 that mutual funds represented 35 million adults in 1985, compared to 10 million in 1980. "Small investors, in short, aren't dead, just changed. Many of them have quit battling the institutions in the market and have joined them."[1] The public has become part of the professionals, the strong hands.

In the corporate realm, *Aunt Janes* and *widows and orphans* populate the stockholders' meetings. An Aunt Jane, sometimes depicted as a little old lady in tennis shoes, owns a small number of shares in a corporation. *Widows and orphans,* a more widely known description of small stockholders, describes conservative

investors said to live on dividends from blue-chip stocks—especially those of utilities—nicknamed **widows and orphans stocks.**
The phrase "widows and orphans" becomes verbal ammunition any time a corporation takes an action that critics see as damaging to small shareholders (as opposed to institutional investors); the critics appeal to the public with a cry about the harm done to poor widows and orphans. *Moody's* magazine in April 1910 complained that, to liberals, "Every rich man is a self-confessed criminal, who has robbed the widows and the orphans."[2]

According to Wall Street lore, the little people left to themselves will make stupid or at best dull trades, but this is nothing to what they will do if solicited. Take the stock market quip "Why go broke? Go public." It suggests that a private corporation on the verge of bankruptcy could easily sell shares to the uninformed public. History bears out that investors (probably including insiders) have bought stock in crazy schemes. In eighteenth-century England, promoters successfully sold stock in a company that made radish oil, which had no known use; in another company to make "The Wheel of Perpetual Motion"; and in one "For Carrying on an Undertaking of Great Advantage but Nobody to Know what it is."

Not surprisingly, the market has adopted an array of terms to describe a person whom a broker can talk into any trade, no matter how stupid, earning himself an easy commission. **Sucker, mullet, lamb, lily,** and **barefoot pilgrims,** they've been called. Unethical brokers have adopted these terms, but so have those criminal types posing as brokers who sell fraudulent securities and commodities, the inhabitants of **boiler rooms.** More of the boiler-room lingo can be found in the chapter titled "Swindles and Scandals."

While **sucker** has had wide use in general slang for over a hundred years, it also has a long tradition in the market. A character in the 1923 novel *Reminiscences of a Stock Market Operator* sets out various grades of suckers:

I discovered . . . suckers differ among themselves to the degree
of experience. The tyro knows nothing, and everybody, including himself, knows it. But the next, or second, grade thinks he
knows a great deal and makes others feel that way too. He is
the experienced sucker, who has studied—not the market itself
but a few remarks about the market made by a still higher grade
of suckers. . . . It is this semisucker rather than the 100 per
cent article who is the real all-the-year-round support of the
commission houses.[3]

Ruthless stock dealers and their underworld counterparts have
baited suckers through the years who, like the freshwater fish that
bear the same name, have swallowed the fraudulent stock schemes
"hook, line and sinker."

From **sucker** comes the phrase **sucker list,** a list of names, telephone numbers, and addresses of people likely to buy worthless
securities. Boiler-room operators have relied heavily on such lists
and paid well to get them; in the 1920s, salesmen in the real
estate and patent medicine businesses also used sucker lists. A
1906 book examined the variety of lists in detail: the $25 to $50
list included "country investors, Methodist and Baptist ministers,
country doctors, . . . teachers; also barbers, waiters, hospital
nurses"; among the suckers likely to spend $100 to $500 were
"college teachers and professors, small Wall Street lambs, Epis-
copal and Presbyterian ministers, mercantile clerks, some country
merchants."[4] Higher-grade lists covered $1,000 to $100,000
investors.

Even the most legitimate brokerage houses rely on telephone
lists for finding new clients. Novice brokers spend their days **dialing and smiling,** as it's called, making cold calls. In fact, the
area in the brokerage that they sit in, an open space filled with
desks, is sometimes nicknamed the **boiler room.**

Sucker lends its name to the **sucker rally,** which occurs when
outsiders acting on rumors bid up the price of a stock that then
collapses, leaving it in their hands, and to the **sucker play,** any
foolish market move that results in heavy losses.

Mullets, suckers with a lot of money, provide easy targets for tax-shelter sellers as well as stockbrokers. Traditionally, doctors and dentists make prime mullets. In the 1959 novel *The Wheeler Dealers* by George Goodman, a wily Texan who sells oil-and-gas tax shelters goes **mulleting** in New York; one chapter opens, "Henry Tyroon had had a good day. He had actually hooked two mullets."[5] By using "hooked," the author plays on the fact that in standard English a mullet is a type of fish, "especially any of several American suckers."

For the past century, stock market **lambs** have roamed the Street—inexperienced investors who followed the crowd like sheep in a flock and lost their money in rigged markets. Use of lamb to mean a person easily cheated goes back to the seventeenth century; it eventually came to mean specifically those who lost in the market. The lambs acted on rumors, often deliberately started to lure them into deals in which they were **fleeced, sheared,** or **clipped.** They lost the shirts—or wool—off their backs. *To fleece,* in use by the seventeenth century, and *to clip* still mean "to swindle" in general slang. Wall Street called those who sheared the lambs, **wolves,** a term that later came to mean simply "smart operators." A mid-century synonym for **lamb** was **lily,** indicating a "high-brow" sucker; a more recent synonym is the picturesque **barefoot pilgrim,** who has lost his shoes as well as his shirt.

Although Wall Street today may harm small investors, it doesn't compare to the days when lambs were led to the slaughter in droves each time big manipulators cornered the market. In his 1902 novel *The Pit,* Frank Norris warned amateurs away from the commodities market by describing it in lurid terms:

> The [brokerage] firm had no consideration for the "outsiders," "the public"—the Lambs. The Lambs! Such a herd, timid, innocent, feeble, as much out of place in La Salle Street as a puppy in a cage of panthers; the Lambs, whom Bull and Bear did not so much as condescend to notice, but who, in their mutual struggle of horn and claw, they crushed to death by the mere rolling of their bodies.[6]

THE BROKER'S CHANGING IMAGE

Brokers themselves have received as much verbal abuse as they have dished out to the public. "I do not regard a broker as a member of the human race," wrote Balzac in 1841. Today the comments run to "If brokers are so smart, how come they're not rich?" and "A Wall Street professional is just an amateur with a Quotron machine on his desk."

Perhaps the most tenacious of the brokers' image problems has been an association with shady dealing. For years, Wall Street has been fighting this shady image, consciously using language to improve the public's perception of brokers. Unlike slang, the manufactured, respectable names for brokers tend to be long and dull. In the 1950s, Charles Merrill came up with "account executives" to make brokers sound businesslike, while the New York Stock Exchange promoted "registered representatives." In the early 1980s, when brokerage houses began to sell much more than stocks and bonds, brokers became "total financial planners" and "financial consultants" in the jargon.

Broker, the term that customers most frequently use, originally referred to a wine retailer who "broached" or tapped wine casks. It came to mean a middleman and then a financial agent. One early meaning of broker, as "pimp" or "bawd," gives a historical perspective to the seamy associations with the profession.

The other most common name, although it has lost popularity in recent years, is **customer's man.** The phrase emphasizes that the broker serves the customer, but one of the most timeworn jokes on the Street mocks such a notion.

> Once a visitor from out of town was being shown the splendors of the New York financial district. When the tourist and his guide arrived at the Battery, the guide pointed out the elegant ships docked there and said, "Look, those are the brokers' yachts." In his naiveté, the out-of-town man asked, "But where are the customers' yachts?"

(The yachts sometimes belong to bankers, depending on who is telling the joke.)

A fashionably dressed customer's man, whose upper-class appearance would make him appear at home on a yacht, was known in the 1930s and 1940s as an *Airedale,* from the aristocratic image of the canine Airedale. The Airedale's expense account, according to Mencken, was his *front-money.*

Female brokers, once known as *customer's ladies* and *customer's women,* have occupied a place on Wall Street for longer than most people realize. In the 1920s, when women began to invest in a big way, some brokerage firms opened offices exclusively for the *ladybulls,* as Will Rogers called female investors. A slang term in England for female speculators—at one time used in the U.S.— is *mudhens,* which the unabridged edition of *The Random House Dictionary of the English Language* defines as "any of various marsh-inhabiting birds."

Wall Street produced imaginative slang in the 1960s that glamorized brokers without implying associations with the underworld. While go-go dancers were performing in discotheques, *go-go brokers* were performing in the market. *Go-go* comes from the French phrase *à gogo* to mean "in a joyful manner; to your heart's content; galore." On the financial scene, *go-go managers* of *go-go funds,* previously known as *adrenaline funds,* ran mutual funds that purchased high-risk, *go-go stock* for potentially high profits. Wall Street crowned Gerald Tsai of Fidelity Fund as king of the go-go managers; the fact that Tsai was an Asian-American—he was known on the Street as *The Chinaman*—lent him a mystical aura that captured the public's fancy in years when Eastern religion and Nehru shirts appealed to the masses. During the *go-go years* of 1966 to 1969, the market and its inhabitants soared in a joyful manner with glamour stocks and high fliers, creating a legendary time chronicled by John Brooks in his book *The Go-Go Years: When Prices Went Topless.*

In that era, *gunslinger* and *hipshooter* added a macho note to the slang. Like their go-go counterparts, these swinging brokers and fund managers bought and sold volatile stocks at a quick pace, claiming that there was "too much risk in being out of the market." Those managing funds often took a cut of the earnings, rather than a salary, to profit from the risk. They tended to be young and hip, sporting sideburns, wide ties, and an abundance of self-confidence. The western labels portrayed them as quick-at-the-draw, aggressive cowboys, while the stock market's buoyancy made them look brilliant. But they disappeared from sight when the market plummeted, giving credence to the Wall Street wisdom that "When the market's going up, everyone looks smart. Never confuse brains with a bull market."

LAME DUCKS, PLUNGERS, AND HOGS: TYPES OF SPECULATORS

As long as the gunslingers made money, they appeared to be shrewd investors, but looking back after their losses, they seem more like crazy speculators. On Wall Street it's said that the difference between an investor and a speculator is profit: if you make a profit, you've invested—if you take a loss, you've speculated. Or more succinctly, "It's not gambling if you're winning."

In the late 1700s on London's Exchange Alley, the British equivalent of Wall Street, an investor who had speculated and lost was ridiculed as a *lame duck* who had *to waddle out of the alley* and could not return until he paid his debts. Nearly one hundred years before Frank Norris's warning to the lambs, a writer cautioned in a light tone:

> *If to the Stock Exchange you speed*
> *To try with bulls and bears your luck*
> *'Tis odds you soon from gold are freed*
> *And waddle forth a limping duck.*

The expression *lame duck* moved to Wall Street where it was joined by *dead duck,* a speculator who had lost everything and could not even limp along. These descriptions persisted on the

Street through the 1940s. In the underworld in the 1930s, dishonest bankers or stockbrokers dubbed **alley waddlers** defrauded customers at **lame duck exchanges.** (*Lame duck* entered the language of American politics around 1863 to describe an elected official who has lost an election but has time left to serve in the term.)

Among the other players on Wall Street are **hogs** or **pigs,** about whom a much-repeated maxim says, "Bulls make money, bears make money, but hogs lose" (or "pigs lose"). Not satisfied with a modest gain, a hog waits to gross a larger profit every time. But during the wait, the market may fall, leaving the hog with a loss. There is no shortage of hogs in the market where, they say, the two main emotions are greed and despair.

Greed and despair beset another speculator, the **plunger,** an old term for one who takes big risks. This player **takes a plunge** without testing the water first by investigating the stock. Some consider Jesse Livermore, nicknamed the **Boy Plunger,** to have been the greatest plunger of all time; he made a million dollars by selling short during the Panic of 1907, but lost the million within a year in the cotton market. His fortunes roller-coasted in classic plunger style until 1941 when he took his own life.

Even when they are losing, plungers have little patience for their opposites in the market, the **scalpers,** who historically trade small quantities of stocks quickly on small price movements, adhering to the adage "You can't go broke taking small profits." Most often, scalpers are floor brokers or traders, since an outsider's small profits would disappear in brokers' commissions. In today's commodity markets, scalpers still trade on small point movements but some of them trade in quantities so large that the profits or losses equal those of plungers. **Scalping** or **scalping the market** dates back to 1886. (*Scalper* in the sense of "one who took his enemy's scalp" was in the language by 1760, and the theater ticket *scalper* by 1869.)

Scalping of another variety occurs when a brokerage firm finds itself with an undesirable stock and has its brokers recommend it to customers while the firm dumps its own holdings on the market. A broker may deliberately arrange this scenario, buying the stock, promoting it so the price goes up, then selling for a profit—an unethical practice at best.

Two of Wall Street's synonyms for *scalper* also mean "gambler" in general slang. *Punter,* a term from the turn of the century still used in England, and *piker* both mean a small-scale speculator or a small-time gambler. *Punter* came originally from card games in which a player "punts" against the bank; the word was transferred to describe a professional speculator on horses or stocks. Folk etymology traces *piker* to farmers from Pike County, Missouri, who migrated West where they gained a reputation for betting small stakes in card games. *Eighth-chasers,* named such because stock points rise in eighths, and the more up-to-date *in-and-out traders,* also seek small, quick profits.

Bargain hunters have frequented Wall Street since the turn of the century searching for cheap securities said to be on the *bargain counter.* Some market analysts credit the bargain hunters with eliminating weakness in the market by purchasing a stock as soon as its price declines.

Wall Street has also long been home to the small operator, once known as a *tailor* or *tailer,* who rides on the coat-tails of market leaders. When manipulation dominated the exchanges, small speculators would *coat-tail the market* by following the lead of the successful pool operators. But big-time manipulators Daniel Drew and Jay Gould delighted in undermining the coat-tailers by dropping *poisoned tips.* Legend relates that Gould once gave a tip on Pacific Mail to the minister of a wealthy congregation, promising to make up losses if the tip proved wrong. As Gould had anticipated, the minister passed the tip on to his rich parishioners; Pacific Mail dropped and Gould paid the minister's losses. When told that the parishioners had lost heavily on the tip, Gould reveled in the news, saying, "They were the people I was after."

In today's market, coat-tailing occurs when stockholders benefit from corporate raiders, as described in a *New York Times* article with the subheading "A Tale of Coattails."[7] Using a similar metaphor, the 1980s slang term *tailgating* refers to the discreditable practice of a broker who follows the lead of a knowledgeable customer, buying or selling stock that the customer does.

THE VENERABLE BULLS AND BEARS

And all this out of Change-Alley? Every shilling, Sir; all out of Stocks, Tuts, Bulls, Rams, Bears, and Bubbles.

The slang words **bull** and **bear** secured a place in the market lexicon early on, as seen in this 1721 quotation from playwright Colley Cibber and London's Exchange Alley. **Bear,** which dates to 1709 as market slang in England, describes an investor who believes that prices are going to fall and invests accordingly. Bears usually **sell short,** selling stocks they do not own in the hope that by the time they must deliver the stock to the buyer, the price will have dropped and they can make a profit on the difference. A bull optimistically believes that the market is going up and so buys stock, taking the **long** position, and expects to sell later at a profit.

Bear has prompted several folk etymologies. One suggests that, since a market bear seeks to depress prices, the name comes from the verb *to bear*, meaning to "press heavily upon." According to another theory, it comes from *bare*, because a bear has sold short stocks he does not own and so is "bare" of stocks. British slang at the turn of the century to describe someone who had sold short was **bear of stocks.**

The most widely held explanation attributes the market term *bear* to the old proverb "Don't sell the bearskin before the bear is caught," about hunters who collected payment for a bearskin before going hunting, then died before delivering the goods. In *Henry V*, Shakespeare refers to a similar proverbial situation regarding lion-hunting:

> *The man that once did sell the lion's skin*
> *While the beast lived, was kill'd with hunting him.*

Since speculators on the London Exchange were called **bear-skin jobbers** in the eighteenth century, probably from the phrase "to sell the bear," this etymology appears the most sound.

Bull may have come into use simply because it was the opposite of **bear.** Slang expert Stuart Flexner explains that **bear** and **bull** were associated in the sport of bear and bull baiting, popular in the eighteenth century, which made *bear and bull* a common phrase.[8] Others suggest that because bulls on the farm lift things up with their horns, they gave their name to the market bulls who lift up prices.

Whatever their origins, the two words have pervaded stock market slang for more than three centuries, during which Wall Streeters have delighted in extending the nouns **bull** and **bear** into other parts of speech and numerous phrases.

For example, they have expanded **bull** into the adjective **bullish,** which is now part of general slang to mean "optimistic." You may be "bullish on America," having faith in the country's future, without investing in the stock market. A **bearish** investor, of course, believes the market will go down. An investor can be bearish on one stock and bullish on another, or move from bullish to bearish: losing faith in the market, unloading stocks, and then selling short. They say on the Street, "There's no one so bearish as a sold-out bull."

Traditionally, the public hates bears, who appear to be betting against the country's well-being and profiting at the expense of good citizens. Enemies of these supposedly unpatriotic bears like to quote J. P. Morgan's pronouncement, "Remember, my son, that any man who is a bear on the future of this country will go broke."

When the market is declining, Wall Streeters talk about the **bear market** and tell each other that "bear markets separate the boys from the men." Since more investors are bulls than bears, the Street prefers a **bull market** with its advancing prices and happier atmosphere. Optimists are quick to spot a **baby bull,** a market where slight rises in price give hope for an imminent bull market. It is commonly held that a bear market begins when everything is brightest and the public is at its most bullish—hence Joseph Kennedy's reaction to the shoeshine boy—while a bull market emerges when all is darkest and the public is deserting the market.

When big operators manipulated the market, they could produce a bull market by *bulling the prices,* also called *bulling the market,* artificially pushing up prices. Some operators specialized in selling short and then *bearing the market,* forcing prices down. Wall Street called the two maneuvers *bull raids* and *bear raids.* Powerful bulls pushed up stock prices during *bull runs* and during the sustained efforts of *bull campaigns,* while *bear campaigns* and *bear drives* forced prices down.

Even today a bear raid—now illegal but not extinct—may cause a *bear panic* or *bear squeeze* (more on squeezes later) as the short sellers run to cover their shorts, performing the frightened steps whimsically called a *bear dance* at the turn of the century.

Speculators once banded together to manipulate the market in organized *bear pools* and *bull pools* led by managers and accompanied by formal agreements about splitting profits. They also joined efforts in *bear cliques* and *bull cliques,* similar but less formal than pools. Professional bulls considered as a whole formed the *bull contingent;* their opposite number was the *bear crowd.* All these battles prompted Wall Streeters at one time to call the exchange floor the *arena of the bears and bulls.*

In the endless permutations of bull and bear, a *stale bull* was one who carried his stock for a long time without a profit, and a *stale bear* was one who had been short of stock for a long time, as recorded in the 1950s. Still, investors would rather grow stale than be trapped. The market sets a *bear trap* when a falling off in prices that encourages short selling is followed by a sharp rise that traps the bears into selling at a loss. The opposite danger, a *bull trap,* is sprung when the market rallies and draws in bullish investors, then fails and traps the bulls—another way of saying *sucker rally.*

ON THE INSIDE

For years an inner circle of players controlled the market and proved true the words of Daniel Drew, "To speculate in Wall Street when you are not an insider is like buying cows by candle-light." Today, Wall Streeters still form a hierarchy, although a less impenetrable one, with the public at the bottom and the mysterious "they" at the top.

Customers rank below brokers, whom they, initially at least, tend to view as important and knowledgeable. Louis Engel wrote of customers,

> They think of the broker as a somewhat forbidding individual who gives his time only to Very Important People, people who are well-heeled and travel in the right social circles.[9]

Brokers see it differently. Within their ranks, a hierarchy puts the *big producers,* who earn large commissions, above their fellow brokers. And beyond brokers are groups closer still to the proverbial "inside." In a technical sense, *insider* means an officer or director, or a person or corporation that owns ten percent or more of the stock of a public company; the SEC requires insiders to report any significant changes in their holdings. Less technically, anyone who has exclusive information about a company and its future actions may be referred to as an insider. The term, which originated around 1830, once meant someone who acted as a broker and traded for his own account, as opposed to an investor who employed a broker.

Rumors on the Street dwell on what the *smart money* is doing, which includes the movements of exchange members, specialists, and other sophisticated investors, otherwise known as the *smart money boys, wise money boys,* or *smart money men.* The smart money, which is sometimes contrasted to the *dumb money,* can be either bullish or bearish. In past years, market commentators referred to the smart money as the Wall Street *talent,* which included the *big operators,* those with the most power in the market.

On the exchange floors, traders look up to *floor animals,* those with an instinct for trading successfully. Another respected character in the commodities exchanges is the *position trader* who buys contracts and holds on to them, which is far riskier than scalping. Since the position trader ends the trading day without closing contracts, fellow traders express admiration with the comment, "He carries a lot of beans home with him." Low in the ranks of prestige at the stock exchanges is the *two-dollar broker,* a broker's broker who transacts orders for member firms when their brokers are too busy or are absent from the floor. The name came from the original fee of $2.00 per one hundred shares traded, now a negotiable fee.

Wall Streeters describe the innermost circle of professionals on or off the floor as simply *they.* This vague term was on the lips of all investors during the 1920s, when the country was caught up in the market; and in the 1980s traders advise, "Watch what they do, not what they say." "They" are the unnamed, mysterious powers thought to be behind the market. In a recent book about commodity traders, the author describes one broken-down trader's perception of they:

> It was always the ubiquitous *they*, those indefinable conspirators who would inevitably force the market to go the opposite way you were playing it. *They* were the rumormongers who forced stock and commodity prices to fluctuate wildly regardless of the economic climate. . . . *They* were the brains, the *real* insiders with all the money to manipulate the markets to make more. . . . *They* were the enemy: heartless; calculating; always on the offensive; forever elusive.[10]

INVESTMENT THEOLOGIES

Just as anyone from a shoeshine boy to a smart money boy can be a bull or bear, anyone can adopt an investment theology and join one of Wall Street's schools of thought, compared by more than one writer to religious beliefs. During the twentieth century, the schools of *fundamentalists, technicians, Random Walkers,* and *contrarians* have espoused methods of understanding and predicting the market in general or in a particular stock.

These creeds—especially that of technicians—have the strongest hold on research analysts, those members of brokerage firms known as the *gnomes of Wall Street,* who provide the salespeople with information and predictions. The nickname is modeled on the "Gnomes of Zurich," slang which originated in 1964 for "international bankers and financiers." Research analysts with a talent for math and science, a breed that has gained popularity lately, are known on Wall Street as *rocket scientists.*

Fundamentalists live by the principle "Investigate, then invest." They study a company's record and look at its prospects, while taking into account outside factors such as the economy and the political situation, all in search of a stock that is undervalued. Benjamin Graham, known as the *Father of Security Analysis,* prefaced his book on the fundamental approach with appropriate words from the *Ars Poetica* of Horace:

> *Many shall be restored that now are fallen and many*
> *Shall fall that now are in honor.*[11]

Fundamentalists dominate during bear markets, and the other largest group, technicians, dominate during bull markets.

Technicians, also called *chartists,* keep charts of market and stock movements, and make decisions based on the patterns on the charts. These market players assume that the price of a stock reflects its worth, making it pointless to search for undervalued stocks. Some say that technicians care more about charts than profits, hence the street saying that "Technicians don't live in Palm Beach," a variant of Bernard Baruch's comment, "Bears don't live on Park Avenue." Chartists have developed a specialized vocabulary to describe the patterns, employing terms such as *head and shoulders, island reversal, runaway gap,* and *diaper indicator.* The language dates back at least to the turn of the century, when charts included *double tops* and *double bottoms.*

A third school adopts the *Random Walk Theory,* which rose

to prominence in the 1960s. The popularized explanation of it is that throwing darts at the financial page works as well as any other method for selecting stocks. A story, told in several versions, immortalized the theory:

> In 1967 a senator from New England (some say an economist at Yale) pinned a *Wall Street Journal* stock report to the wall and hurled darts at it to prove that mutual fund managers could have improved their performance in picking stocks with this approach. He then invested a hypothetical $10,000 in the random stocks, using statistics from the last ten years to calculate how his imaginary portfolio would have done, and came out ahead of any mutual fund.

It has become a cliché for investors who lose money by following their brokers' advice to complain that they could have done as well by throwing darts at the stock listings.

Wall Street has taken contrariness and elevated it to an investment theology, that of the **contrarian** who likes to act opposite to the dominant mood in the market. "Buy when others are selling, sell when they buy," a proverb attributed to Bernard Baruch, describes the contrarian's method, which rejects another piece of proverbial advice, "The trend is your friend." Some contrarians claim that they don't buy until "the blood is running in the streets," from the legend about one of the Comtes de Rothschild who, when asked how he made his money in the French stock market, said, "When the streets of Paris are running with blood, I buy." In this story and the entire contrarian method, Wall Streeters once again assert that the so-called public, those amateur investors whose blood runs during a panic, is likely to be wrong.

4

Kings and Queens, Wizards and Witches: Nicknames for People

MODERN MONIKERS

People in all aspects of Wall Street—from the exchanges to brokerages to investment banking—and in all parts of the country, sport colorful nicknames. At the investment banking firm of Lazard Frères in New York, Felix Rohatyn gained fame for his role as chairman of New York's Municipal Assistance Corporation, which was organized to keep the city from bankruptcy, and Wall Street dubbed him *Felix the Fixer, Wizard of Lazard.* On the West Coast resides the former *Mighty Mouse of Block Trading,* Boyd Jefferies, who was ousted from the market after being found guilty of two felony charges.

Traders on the exchange floors have gained nicknames of all varieties: *Harry the Hat, Tijuana Tube Man, Bambi, Plastic Man, the Barracuda, King Cole,* and *Shamu the Killer Whale*—a former football player. Occasionally friends on the floor will be called by a joint name, such as two former basketball players nicknamed

The World Trade Center, and another set of two traders, one called **Rock** and the other **Roll.** These are but a few of many.

Sometimes it's easy to see why a certain name arose. In the 1950s, Sidney Weinberg of Goldman, Sachs gained a worldwide reputation for his influence in the market, earning him the sobriquet of **Mr. Wall Street.** Dean Witter's Robert Gardiner became **Stretch** and Paul Volcker, formerly of the Federal Reserve, **Tall Paul,** because of their height. In an oral-history edition of *Institutional Investor,* June 1987, Henry Kaufman, chief economist at Salomon Brothers, mused about his nickname:

> I think that reputation I picked up of being Dr. Gloom came into being because I had these bearish views during relatively long periods in which the bond markets acted adversely. I never felt good about being called Dr. Gloom, but I never worried about it, either, because I think you should try to say it as it is.[1]

The takeover game has nurtured the art of nicknaming among Wall Streeters. In the 1960s, they christened James Ling the **Merger King,** and Charles Bluhdorn of Gulf & Western the **Mad Austrian,** from his country of birth and his approach to takeovers. William Tavoulareas of Mobil Corporation was the first in a line of raiders known by their enemies as **Jaws,** likening him to the killer shark in the movie *Jaws.* For his practice of acquiring financially troubled companies and then selling them off piece by piece, Irwin Jacobs has been cynically dubbed **Irv the Liquidator,** playing on the two meanings of "liquidate": to dissolve a corporation and to murder someone.

Wall Street nicknamed Michael Milken of Drexel Burnham the **Junk Bond King** for his role in engineering a new use for junk bonds in financing hostile takeovers. When Ivan Boesky, nicknamed among other things **Ivan the Pig** or **Piggy,** agreed to pay $100 million as a result of his insider trading, Wall Streeters joked about Milken's junk bonds:

> Did you hear that Boesky will only have to come up with $5 million of the $100 million SEC fine? Apparently Drexel

Burnham is "highly confident" they can raise the other ninety-five with junk bonds.

Another widely publicized insider trading scandal featured the **Yuppie Five**—two arbs, one lawyer, one stockbroker, and one customer. The five men traded on inside information about takeovers, gleaned by the lawyer, until the SEC caught up with them. The youth and self-indulgent lifestyle of these men, all in their twenties, inspired their nickname, from the currently popular slang word "yuppie" for "young urban professional."

THE LOBSTER AND THE WHITE ELEPHANT

The habit of nicknaming among Wall Streeters has a long history. In 1873, when William Fowler wrote about his fellow brokers, he liked to comment on their nicknames. For one broker, **Little Bitters** "was the name under which he was known among his Wall Street associates, though why he should have borne this name it is hard to say."[2] A retired physician, a market bear, bore the title **Ursa Minor,** Latin for "little bear" and one name for the Little Dipper constellation. His exploits as a short seller paled in comparison to brighter market stars such as Addison Commack and Daniel Drew, each known as **Ursa Major.**

Fowler and his friends knew one broker as **The Lobster,** "so called from his very red face and bulging eyes," and a few years later, according to John Moody, Wall Streeter Stuyvesant Fish also took his nickname from his appearance:

> Fish was a big, open-faced, easy-mannered young man, whose blond hair and great stature had earned for him in the financial district the name of "White Elephant."[3]

In 1916, A Short Story of the New York Stock Exchange supplied a whole list of nicknames from the recent past, but without any explanations for their origins. The reader today is left to puzzle over why John B. Colgate was **Roast Beef Rare** or why Charles

Noyes was **Charlie Vapor.** One can guess at William Pearl's nickname of **Dr. Smooth,** and can surmise that Robert Goodbody gained the name **Turrible Things** from favoring that phrase in conversation. James Barnes was dubbed **Pocket-Book Jimmie,** E. N. Nichols was **Captain Swift,** and Henry Clews, a writer whose reminiscences of Wall Street are quoted in these pages, was known as **Louis the Sixteenth.** The nickname for Edmund Stedman poses no problems, for history notes his role on Wall Street, and anthologies still contain his poems, explaining the name of **The Banker-Poet.**[4]

Chicago traders did their share of nicknaming as well. For example, in the 1870s, they had their **King Jack,** William Sturges, and, around the turn of the century, their **King of the Bucket Shops,** C. C. Christie. A notorious and powerful speculator in the late nineteenth century, still remembered, was **Old Hutch,** Benjamin P. Hutchinson. Known for his vast skill at manipulating the commodities market, he even gave his name to a fall in the futures market, known as the **Old Hutch Panic.**

Most of the nicknames recorded in Wall Street's history applied, not to small-time operators, but to the market greats. Just as so-called wizards and kings inhabit today's markets, the big speculators in the past received grandiose nicknames. In the years before and after the turn of the century, a group of these important figures took on a name, collectively, from Greek mythology, and became known as the **Titans of Finance.** The mythological Titans had enormous strength and stature; they wielded—and often abused—immense power. Except for the fact that, according to Hesiod, six of the Titans were female and the other six male, the analogy of Wall Street powers to the Greek Titans worked well.

Among stock market gods numbered J. P. Morgan, Edward Harriman, Jay Gould, Daniel Drew, and Cornelius Vanderbilt, all of whom bore individual nicknames as well. These men were constantly battling for financial supremacy, and their cutthroat methods drew a comment from the Irish-American character Mr. Dooley around the turn of the century:

"Well, sir," said Mr. Dooley, "I see th' Titans iv Finance has clutched each other be th' throat an' engaged in a death sthruggle. Glory be, whin business gets above sellin' tinpinny nails in a brown paper cornucopy, 't is hard to tell it fr'm murther."

Mr. Dooley, created by parodist Peter Finley Dunne, goes on to say, "A Ti-tan iv Fi-nance is a man that's got more money thin he can carry without bein' disordherly."[5]

BEWARE OF FINANCIAL NAPOLEONS

For many years, the French emperor Napoleon Bonaparte provided a popular titanic image—and a series of nicknames—for speculators who had conquered the market. Of course, the would-be financial emperors, like their namesake, often ended up in defeat, evoking comparisons to Napoleon's losses at Waterloo and Moscow, or his fate as a British prisoner of war on the island of St. Helena. Thus, a British proverb from the 1920s warns investors: Beware of Financial Napoleons—remember Moscow and St. Helena.

The Gilded Age of the 1890s idolized Napoleon, affectionately dubbed the *Little Corporal*. The biographies of him published in 1894 became best-sellers, and when *McClure's* published a collection of pictures of the hero in 1893, its circulation increased by thirty thousand copies in a month. The hero-worship lasted into the twentieth century, when speculator Serge Rubinstein so fancied the image that he hosted frequent costume parties during the 1940s at which he always dressed as Napoleon.

Napoleons of the market have cropped up in fiction as well as real life. In his short story "The Man Who Won," Edwin Lefevre has a character known as the *Napoleon of the Street*, and one of Frank Norris's characters, a Chicago tycoon, is the *Napoleon of LaSalle Street*.[6]

Ferdinand Ward, not a fictional character but as despicable as any storybook villain, so impressed Wall Street when he first made his appearance that his colleagues called him the **Young Napo-**

leon of Finance. Ward formed a brokerage partnership with President Ulysses S. Grant after Grant had left the White House, and he attracted customers who trusted the former president. The so-called Napoleon proceeded to speculate disastrously, ruining Grant's reputation, landing himself in prison, and setting off the panic of 1884, known as the **Grant & Ward Crash.**

In the nineteenth century, Addison Jerome was called the **Napoleon of the Public Board,** because he dominated that exchange, which was organized in the 1860s. Jerome, a great-uncle of Winston Churchill, made millions through speculation, but his Waterloo took the form of attempting unsuccessfully to corner Michigan Southern railroad. He died shortly afterward in poverty.

A short man like the Little Corporal, the powerful Edward Henry Harriman became known as the **Little Napoleon of the Railroads,** but only after he had held the title of the **Little Wizard of Wall Street.** Harriman's career began at the age of fourteen when he served as a broker's messenger boy, where he learned the ways of Wall Street; he made his first big profit by selling short before a panic, and used it to buy a seat on the Exchange. After marrying into the Averill family, which owned a small railroad, Harriman began to build the railroad empire that earned him the title of Napoleon.

Another who ascended to the Wall Street throne was Jacob Little, considered by market historian Robert Sobel to have been the first original mind in the stock market, the Street's first real leader, and its first significant full-time professional. James Medbery wrote in 1871 about one of Little's Napoleonic exploits, when he had sold Erie stock short.

> Every broker in the Board combined against him. On settlement day, as the story goes, he walked up Wall Street with serene countenance, while the joy of expectant disaster gleamed darkly and scornfully at him from a hundred eyes. He had been long known as the Napoleon of the Exchange, and all the brokers said that two o'clock would be his Waterloo.[7]

In fact, Little, who had foreseen the battle, knew he could defeat his enemies by converting bonds he secretly held into shares of Erie stock. His prowess at short selling made him the current *Great Bear of Wall Street* and the fortunes he acquired crowned him, for a time, as the *King of Wall Street.* But he lost it all and, like so many market greats, died poor, once again giving credence to the Wall Street saying, "The speculator who dies rich dies before his time."

The same title of king and the same fate of dying poor characterized another speculator, Anthony Morse. Once "the most dashing operator ever known in Wall Street," according to William Fowler in his 1873 book *Inside Life in Wall Street,* Morse's reign as king was short, and he too lost his fortune, bringing others down with him. Fowler commented,

> His end speaks to all like a warning voice. He departed from the arena, a stripped, penniless, heart-stricken man. Out of the troops of wealthy friends which but lately clustered about him, only one or two still clung to him. He had now only the shadow of a great name.[8]

THE BEARISH UNCLE DAN'L

Jacob Little goes down in history as the first *Great Bear of Wall Street,* but his successor Daniel Drew qualifies as the most famous one. Drew's life, which provided the stuff of legends, began in 1797 on a farm in upstate New York. As his first business venture, he drove cattle to market, and then ran a steamboat company on the Hudson, where he so annoyed Cornelius Vanderbilt with his price-cutting that Vanderbilt bought him out.

In 1844 Drew opened a brokerage office on Wall Street but eventually confined his trading to his own account. Although nearly illiterate, Drew—like Vanderbilt—kept accurate track of his accounts in his head. He wore a scruffy drover's hat and carried a shabby umbrella even after he had made his fortune, and in response to this rustic persona, Wall Streeters called him **Uncle Daniel,** or the more countrified **Uncle Dan'l.**

Yet another nickname for this eccentric figure was **The Deacon,** reflecting his religious tendencies. Drew was a psalm-singing Methodist who quoted from the Bible, opened his house to any Methodist minister visiting New York, and contributed money to the Drew Theological Seminary. But his religious leanings didn't keep him from taking to the bottle when things went wrong, nor did religious scruples soften his style on Wall Street.

Uncle Dan'l enjoyed deceiving other speculators with what became known as the **handkerchief trick;** he would take out a big white handkerchief to wipe his brow and, as if by accident, would drop a small slip of paper from the handkerchief. After Drew had left the area, men hungry for a tip would rush over and read the slip, apparently a reminder to buy a certain stock or sell one short. But, of course, to follow the poisoned tip brought only losses.

This kind of malicious behavior explains a story Jay Gould liked to tell about Drew:

> At one time Drew went into a Methodist Church while a revival was in progress, and listened to a convert telling how sinful he had been—lying, cheating and robbing men of their money in Wall Street. Fascinated by the confession, Drew nudged a neighbor and asked: "Who is he, anyhow?" "That's Daniel Drew," was the reply.[9]

Both Drew and Gould played major roles in the ongoing struggle over the Erie Railroad and its stock, known as the **Erie Wars.** Gould, once Drew's partner, turned against him and eventually gained the upper hand, sending Drew to financial ruin. No wonder Drew said of Gould, "His touch is Death."

WIZARD AND DEVIL

The Mephistopheles of Wall Street they called Jay Gould, with his devilish tricks and his vast power. He was so widely disliked that when he died, *The New York Times* commented,

With the announcement of Mr. Gould's death it was to be expected that there would be demonstrations indicating something else than regret—for hatred of Jay Gould has been the principal tenet of many a Wall Street creed.

One reason for the hatred was that Gould, together with James Fisk, triggered the market panic on **Black Friday,** September 24, 1869, when they came just short of cornering gold. In his wizardly way, even in defeat, Gould arranged to emerge with a profit.

Sometimes his enemies tried cunning schemes similar to Gould's own to outsmart him, but they seldom succeeded. However, one story of success is told. In 1881, a storm blew down telegraph wires, forcing Gould to rely on messenger boys to deliver his financial communications. Two brokers kidnapped one of his messengers, and replaced him with one of similar appearance. For weeks, they intercepted Gould's messages and wreaked havoc on his trading, until he discovered the trick.

No matter how much his contemporaries hated Gould, they couldn't deny his power in the market, and he was freely acknowledged to be the **Wizard of Wall Street.** When he wasn't seeing to his railroads or manipulating the market, this Titan of the market spent his time harmlessly cultivating orchids in the greenhouse of his country home. He died in 1892 at the age of fifty-eight, reportedly leaving a fortune of seventy million dollars.

JUBILEE JIM FISK

For sheer color, Gould couldn't hold a candle to his partner on Black Friday, **Jubilee Jim** Fisk, "a depraved and dissolute ruffian who kept a harem at the Opera House, and delighted in driving about the streets in a chariot full of loose women, drawn by six prancing steed," according to the *Review of Reviews* in 1894.[10]

Legend has it that James Fisk worked in a circus early in his life, and he cultivated a circuslike aspect to his later years; hence, one of his many nicknames, the **Barnum of Wall Street.** Fisk acquired a fortune during the Civil War by selling Confederate bonds in England, then worked for Daniel Drew, who enlisted him as an officer in the so-called Erie Wars. When Pike's Opera House, which Fisk owned and where he produced light opera, became a center for the Erie operation, Wall Streeters dubbed it *Erie Castle* while they called its owner the *Prince of Erie.*

With the kind of extravagance that gained him so much publicity, the showy prince liked to dress in a resplendent admiral's uniform on board his luxury ship, the SS *Providence*, flagship of the Narragansett Steamship Line, of which Fisk was president. This nautical bent prompted yet another nickname, *Admiral Fisk.*

Even his death had an air of exaggeration. Fisk's mistress, the actress Josie Mansfield, fell in love with a younger man, Ned Stokes, who blackmailed Fisk with compromising letters that Jubilee Jim had written to the actress. When Fisk decided to quit paying, Mansfield brought a suit against him. After one of the days in court, Stokes ambushed Fisk at the Grand Central Hotel and shot him on the hotel's grand staircase. Fisk died from the wounds and lay in state at the opera house, followed by an appropriately splendid funeral for Jubilee Jim.

THE COMMODORE AND HIS PUPS

During the wars over the Erie Railroad, Drew, Gould, and Fisk banded together to do battle with one of the richest men in the world, Cornelius Vanderbilt, better known as *Commodore Vanderbilt.* The nickname came from the days when the young Vanderbilt ran a steamboat ferry for freight and passengers from Staten Island to Manhattan. He expanded it into a shipping line, then added railroads to his holdings to build up a vast financial empire. That the Commodore wielded enormous power over the stock market emerges in William Fowler's 1873 description of him as

buying with a lordly manner, thousands and tens of thousands of shares, punishing his enemies with a remorseless hand, and

placing his adversaries hors du combat, or sitting like a gener-
alissimo in his office, issuing his orders to his battalions.[11]

Wall Streeters called his battalions of brokers the *Commodore's pups,* whom he employed to carry out his trading orders,
execute his battle plans, and punish his enemies. His remorseless
hand emerges in a letter he once wrote to two associates who had
crossed him:

> Gentlemen, You have undertaken to cheat me. I won't sue
> you, for the law is too slow. I'll ruin you.
>
> [Signed] C. Vanderbilt.

A cagey operator, Vanderbilt attributed his success to the policy
"Never tell anyone what you are going to do till you've done it."
His methods worked so well for him that when he died in 1877,
Wall Streeters believed the Commodore to be the richest man in
the world, and well deserving of his nickname *Old Eighty Mil-
lions.*

Shrewd as he was in business, when it came to his health,
Vanderbilt succumbed to superstitions, placing saltcellars under
his bed as "health conductors," and consulting with two sisters
who, through his influence, caused quite a stir on Wall Street.
The sisters were Tennessee Claflin, known as a faith healer, and
her sister Victoria Woodhull, later the first woman to run for
President of the United States.

WOMEN BEWITCH WALL STREET

In 1870, the sisters opened the first all-female brokerage in the
country, Woodhull, Claflin & Co., at 44 Broad Street in New
York. So many Wall Streeters flocked to the office to stare at the
reportedly beautiful women, quickly nicknamed the *Lady Brokers*
and the *Bewitching Brokers,* that the brokerage finally posted a
sign which read, "All gentlemen will state their business and then
retire at once."

Magazines and newspapers had a heyday at the expense of the

newly crowned **Queens of Finance.** For example, the *Cleveland Leader* voiced its disapproval of Woodhull in strong words, condemning "her brazen immodesty as a stock speculator in Wall Street." A cartoon in *The New York Telegraph*, February 18, 1870, pictured the sisters in a cart pulled by bulls and bears with men's faces; the caption read "The Lady Brokers Driving the Bulls and Bears of Wall Street. Tennie C. Holding the Reins, Victoria the Whip." Fallen bodies lie around the cart, and ducks with crutches stand nearby, referring to the slang expression **lame ducks** and implying that Woodhull and Claflin were financially ruining their brokerage customers. The next month a cartoon ran in *Harper's Weekly* captioned "The Bewitching Brokers—Women on 'Change,'" depicting three women pulling at the clothes of a struggling man, erroneously implying that the exchange was about to be overrun with female brokers.

Henry Clews, writing in 1888, drew a pessimistic conclusion about any woman's chances in the market:

> My knowledge of the history of those sisters and their financial relations and business connections with the late Commodore Vanderbilt, go to illustrate the fact very clearly that the cleverest women cannot be successful in Wall Street.

He goes on to advise that "It is probably only in the matrimonial line that women can become successful speculators."[12]

While conducting their brokerage business, the sisters also published the *Woodhull & Claflin's Weekly,* a newspaper with 20,000 subscribers. In it, they advocated women's suffrage, sex education, free love, and socialism, and eventually turned to exposing corruption and graft. It embroiled them in lawsuits, during which their brokerage business suffered until it closed its doors for the last time in 1872, the same year that Woodhull ran for President with Frederick Douglass as her running partner.

Although Henry Clews believed women did not belong on Wall Street, he admitted one exception to the rule, Hetty Green, nicknamed the **Witch of Wall Street.** He commented that her "unaided sagacity has placed her among the most successful of our millionaire speculators," but explained that, "She is, however, made up of a powerful masculine brain in an otherwise female constitution, and is one among a million of her sex."[13]

Born Henrietta Howland Robinson, she inherited six million dollars from her father and aunt, and increased it through market manipulations in railroad stocks at the NYSE, where she was the first and only female operator. Due to her brilliant financial maneuvers, when she died, the Witch of Wall Street left one hundred million dollars and a reputation as the greatest woman financier of her time.

Unlike Woodhull and Claflin, Hetty Green repulsed rather than charmed Wall Street with her looks and style of living. Despite her wealth, she lived in dingy boarding houses and cheap flats, and cooked her own meals. A reporter for the *New York Tribune* described her witchlike appearance on May 27, 1886:

> Mrs. Green wore what once had been a black dress, which must have been of practically indestructible material. It turned brown, then green, and still she wore it; and carried an umbrella and handbag of about the same era as her dress.

He went on,

> In Mrs. Green's handbag, she carried graham crackers—bought in bulk—on which she munched from time to time remarking she was thus saved from paying the "prohibitive prices" of New York's restaurants.

A KING AND A GOD

Russell Sage, a contemporary of Hetty Green's, started in the grocery business in upstate New York, then moved his focus to New York City, where he became known as the *Money King of Wall Street.* Financial institutions turned to Sage when they needed loans, for the Money King liked to claim, "I keep more ready money than any bank." A powerful force in railroads, Sage served as president of at least twenty railroad corporations.

His other nickname, the **Father of Puts and Calls,** credits him with devising put and call options, also known in those days as *privileges,* which he manipulated with masterly skill. Rumor told that he made ten million dollars in just one month through puts and calls. Sage died in 1906, leaving his wife temporarily the wealthiest woman into the world, until she established the Russell Sage Foundation with part of the fortune in 1907.

Most legendary of all the Titans of Finance was John Pierpont Morgan, whose high-handed manner and immense power earned him another nickname from mythology: **Jupiter,** from the Roman king of the gods.

J. P. Morgan, who lived from 1837 to 1913, built up the Morgan empire, battling such Wall Street greats as Jay Gould, James Fisk and E. H. Harriman along the way. As one of his financial ventures, he consolidated approximately three-fifths of the country's steel business under one management, in a process dubbed *morganization,* which Mr. Dooley had something to say about in his Irish brogue:

> Pierpont Morgan calls in wan iv his office boys, th' prisidint iv a national bank, an' says he, "James," he says, "take some change out iv th' damper an' r-run out an' buy Europe f'r me," he says. "I intind to reorganize it an' put it on a paying basis," he says. "Call up the Czar an' th' Pope an' th' Sultan an' th' Impror Willum, an' tell thim we won't need their savices afther nex' week," he says. "Give thim a year's salary in advance."

His apparently infallible domination over American business provoked a visiting archbishop from England to nickname him **Pierpontifex Maximus,** while Wall Streeters bestowed on Morgan and his twelve business partners at the House of Morgan the most extravagant and irreverent of titles, **Jesus Christ and his Twelve Apostles.** Even Morgan's apostles became the stuff of Wall Street folklore. In the 1890s, the business partners at the **House on the Corner,** as the firm was called, so impressed Wall Streeters with their good looks that they coined the saying, "When the angels of God took unto themselves wives among the daughters of men, the result was the Morgan partners." But, on the debit side, Wall Streeters also shared a belief that, though handsome, the Morgan apostles tended to die young from too much work.

Two remarks by the elder J. P. Morgan, whose son also bore that name, have been handed down in market history. The **Great Man,** as he was called, often growled—and many have since repeated—"I'm not on Wall Street for my health." The other much-quoted line came in answer to frequently asked questions about what he thought the market would do; Morgan would always reply, unarguably, "It will fluctuate."

THE WALDORF CROWD

In his 1957 autobiography, *Baruch: My Own Story*, financier Bernard M. Baruch introduced readers to a group of Wall Streeters known as the **Waldorf Crowd.** Baruch, born in 1870, gained a fortune through speculation by the time he reached thirty years old. During the first years of this century, he and other Wall Street characters gathered most days after the Exchange closed at the Waldorf-Astoria hotel, then located where the Empire State Building now stands. There, wrote Baruch, one might come across Mark Twain, Lillian Russell, Gentleman Jim Corbett, "countless presidents of banks and railroads," and three of the most colorful stock market speculators: **Diamond Jim** Brady, John **Bet-A-Million** Gates, and James R. Keene, the **Silver Fox.**

No Wall Street character was more aptly named than James Buchanan Brady, with his title of Diamond Jim. He amassed great wealth through his sales ability, and began to collect diamonds and other jewels, a collection eventually worth more than one million dollars. Richard Wyckoff described Brady's visits to the brokerage where Wyckoff worked:

> One of our customers in both stocks and cotton was Diamond Jim Brady, who came in frequently and took away with him $25,000 or $50,000 in high-grade bonds or gilt-edge stocks. Diamond Jim was evidently making money in his own business

which was railroad supplies. . . . The diamonds Jim wore would be in harmony with the day's activities. One day his cravat would bear a diamond locomotive and the studs would be railroad cars. Another day it would be a diamond horse that galloped on his tie, while horseshoe studs were in his shirt.[14]

Both Wyckoff and Baruch described Diamond Jim's other extraordinary characteristic, his enormous appetite. One cited the example of Brady's eating a whole punch bowl full of lettuce hearts at one sitting, the other told how he would consume oranges by the dozen and ice cream by the quart.

The stories about John Warne Gates, better known as Bet-A-Million, also paint the picture of extravagance, but rather than diamonds and food, his weakness was gambling, on the market and everywhere else. When the exchange was closed, he would play bridge at the Waldorf-Astoria, for "ten a point." One story tells of a young man who joined the game, believing that the "ten" stood for ten cents, and only realized his mistake when he won and Gates paid him thirty-three thousand dollars.

Bet-A-Million, who made his money in the West by manufacturing barbed-wire fencing, gambled at horse races, pool, whist, faro, poker, and roulette. A well-known legend tells that, one morning on a train, he whiled away the hours by betting on the raindrops as they trickled down the train window, wagering a thousand dollars—some say five thousand dollars—a race.

Gates gets credit for composing a little ditty that mocked the way big operators, of which he was certainly one, so often double-crossed each other:

> The tarantula jumped on the centipede's back
> And chortled with ghoulish glee:
> "I'll poison this murderous son of a gun,
> If I don't he'll poison me!"

Quieter in nature but also a wily gambler at heart, James Keene with his neatly trimmed gray beard was known on Wall Street as the Silver Fox. Baruch, no mean operator himself, paid Keene his highest compliment when he wrote, "No one I ever knew approached him in his skill at operating in the market." According to Baruch, Keene encapsulated his attitude toward life and the market when asked why he still speculated even after he had made a fortune. "Why does a dog chase his thousandth rabbit?" he replied. "All life is speculation. The spirit of speculation is born with men."[15]

His spirit of speculation first paid off on some mining stock. He purchased it in California, then was forced by poor health to leave for the East Coast. Over a year later, Keene returned West, and found that his stock, bought for a few hundred dollars, was worth $200,000, thanks to the discovery of gold in the mine. After a taste of success on Wall Street, Keene began to speculate "in everything that came along—in wheat, lard, opium and fast horses," according to Henry Clews in 1888.[16] The Silver Fox lost his fortune several times, but always gained it back again.

His nickname was inherited by Frank Bliss, a silver-haired pool operator during the 1920s. This Silver Fox bought and sold more stock, and handled larger blocks of stock, than any floor trader before his time, winning his widest fame for running the pool in Piggly-Wiggly for Jesse Livermore.

FROM SUNSHINE TO SCAPEGOAT

> When the stock market goes down Mr. Morgan, Lamont, Charley Mitchell and Mr. George Baker hold a meeting and let everybody see 'em in this huddle. Then the market perks up. I was just thinking what a great idea it would be if we could just get these boys to room together for six months. There is no telling to what heights the market might go.[17]

The fictional Mr. Dooley had a kindred spirit in comedian Will Rogers, both intent on deflating the egos of powerful Wall Streeters. Rogers made his rooming-together suggestion on October 29, 1929, during the Big Crash. A widely circulated report that these Wall Street leaders had met in a room located just below the Exchange floor gave birth to the story that members of Morgan's firm were looking through a periscope from the basement room to the exchange floor to watch the progress of Morgan stocks in secrecy.

In those days, one of the men Rogers mentioned, Charley Mitchell of National City Bank, enjoyed the nickname of **Sunshine Charley,** but the crash sullied his reputation and turned him into the object of scorn; when he was publicly prosecuted, Mitchell became a **Scapegoat of the Crash.**

SOVEREIGNS AND SUICIDES

After the stock market crashed in 1929, the gallows humor joked that a fleet of top hats could be seen floating down the East River every morning—a wild exaggeration, of course. In fact, the two most famous figures from that era to commit suicide did so years after the Crash.

So prolific were the legends surrounding the Swedish **Match King,** Ivan Kreuger, that when his suicide was announced, yet another unlikely legend spread, that the death was a hoax and that Kreuger had fled from Paris to Sumatra. In his heyday in the 1920s, Kreuger dominated the world production of matches. The United States became enamored of him, making it easy for the Match King to sell $148 million of securities on the American markets. His face appeared on the cover of *Time* during October, 1929, and the magazine reported,

> Kreuger-lore has been eagerly collected. There have been stories of his private island in the North Sea, of his apartments in Manhattan, Paris, Berlin, of his never carrying matches, of the statue of Diana in the courtyard of his home office. Herr Kreuger has all the qualities necessary for the creation of a legend. He is remote; he is powerful; he is—to the anti-monopolist— sinister.[18]

The secrecy that characterized the Match King turned out to mask a gigantic swindle. When his financial desperation drove

him to the disputed suicide in 1932, the stock market dropped
steeply, and the price of Kreuger & Toll stock plummeted from
120 to 1. It emerged that Kreuger had left only $100,000—the
millions had somehow vanished; his empire had collapsed like a
house built out of matchsticks.

Even more legendary in the United States, Jesse Livermore became known early in his career as the *Boy Plunger,* and went on
to be honored as the *King of the Speculators.* He is said to have
inspired the well-known Wall Street novel published in 1923,
Reminiscences of a Stock Operator by Edwin LeFevre, which
combines fiction with instruction on trading techniques. Livermore broke new ground in trading with his realization that a
speculator should concentrate on individual stocks and special situations, rather than approach the market as a whole.

During the great bull market of the 1920s, Livermore, contrary
to his nickname of *King of the Bears,* took long positions, though
he tested the market frequently with short sales. When the crucial
time to be a bear came, in the autumn of 1929, Livermore
launched into massive short selling and reaped huge profits when
the market crashed. However, by 1934, he was filing for bankruptcy due to other failures and misfortunes, and in 1940, he shot
himself in the head in the men's room at the Sherry-Netherland
Hotel in New York.

THE WOLF OF WALL STREET

Another Wall Street character who came to an unhappy end was
widely known as the *Wolf of Wall Street.* His contemporaries
could not be certain of the Wolf's real name, because he adopted
several pseudonyms, but the one he favored was David Lamar,
with Lewis and Levy as other choices.

The New York Times reported his death on January 14, 1934,
on its front page, explaining that early in his career, he

> became known as the "gumshoe man" for James R. Keene,
> broker for financial leaders. Always suave, always resplendent,

he trotted around the city on many mysterious errands and made much money in United States Leather common stock. It was not until about 1901 that Lamar began to get the unfavorable publicity which paved the way for his sobriquet—"Wolf of Wall Street."

In the years that followed, Lamar served two prison terms for unscrupulous bear raids, which had brought him millions of dollars. He served another, short sentence, after he boasted during a Senate investigation that he had often posed as a U.S. Congressman in order to promote his financial schemes. During the First World War, Lamar took part in a treasonous plot and was convicted of fomenting strikes in munitions factories in New York and Connecticut.

SELL-'EM BEN SMITH

Bernard E. Smith gained fortune and fame when others in the market had lost theirs—in 1930, after the crash. Already well known for this on Wall Street, in 1932, Smith's reputation spread further afield through a profile in *The New Yorker* by Matthew Josephson, who wrote:

> He was admired as one of the four or five leading bear operators, and rumors of his bold exploits coursed through all the Street's whispering galleries. The legends of his prowess waxed; finally came tales of how mighty financial interests, European and American, had to turn more and more to this hardboiled Irish broker for guidance through the economic jungle: a latter-day genius, having no school or college degree, no pedigree, no Oxford accent.[19]

Sell-'em Ben's life indeed resembled a rags-to-riches novel, coming as he did from a poor Irish-American family on New York's West Side. He held many jobs along the way, including the classic boyhood job of selling newspapers. Josephson's admiring description of Smith reported that his success came from a combination of thorough research, perseverance, and uncanny intuition about the market. But like other legendary figures, Smith inspired more colorful rumors about how he reached the top. One said that he thrived on raw meat. Another suggested that he sold the whole list of stocks short every time President Hoover made an optimistic speech. Other Wall Streeters chalked it up simply to his bearishness, which Smith voiced in his repeated cry about stocks—the cry that gave him his nickname—heard again and again at the Exchange, "Sell 'em. Sell 'em. They're not worth anything."

5

Buy Low, Sell High: Playing the Market

WALL STREET WISDOM

Don't gamble. Take all your savings and buy some good stock and hold it till it goes up, then sell it. If it don't go up, don't buy it.

With this facetious suggestion, Will Rogers poked fun at the endless advice Wall Streeters spout about how to invest wisely. Along with the slang they have coined to describe trading, market professionals have created numerous proverbs on the subject, some of them no easier to follow than Will Rogers' advice.

One well-worn saying attributed to the English financier David Ricardo counsels, "Cut short your losses, let your profits run." But this deceptively simple formula doesn't tell the listener how to identify losses—a drop of one point? two? ten?—or warn that profits turn quickly into losses. For the investor who employs a broker, to buy a stock and then sell it constitutes a **round trip,** for which the broker charges two commissions, a cost not mentioned in the proverb.

Wall Streeters frequently bandy about the advice, "Buy cheap, sell dear," known as the **Rothschild Rule,** a proverb so hoary that in 1875, a writer called it "the old maxim of 'buying cheap, selling dear.' "[1] Everyone would like to buy at a low price and sell at a high one, but—as Will Rogers' suggestion tells us—it's easier said than done. Even the most sophisticated investors cannot be certain that a stock is on its way up, rather than cresting and about to fall. As one market observer has concluded, investors more often follow the route, "Buy high, sell low, then lie about it."

TAKING A FLUTTER

Armed with advice, inexperienced investors venture into the market to **take a flutter,** making a small speculative purchase. Those with more experience **play the market** on a regular basis, a term in use since the 1920s.

Most market players take **long positions,** buying stocks with hopes that the price will go up. When a client wants to **go long,** her broker sends a market order to the exchange floor, telling the firm's floor broker to buy. Various orders may be sent; for example, a market player may insist on a **fill or kill order,** that is, instructing the broker to fill all of the order at one price or else not fill it at all. If the order goes through and then the price goes down, the position proves to be **long and wrong.**

Certain speculators place their faith in **pure plays,** going long on companies involved in only one pursuit. These market bulls look for an up-and-coming area, then hope to **get in on the ground floor,** a market phrase from the turn of the century, and **ride** the stock up. But someone who waits too long, and gets in on a stock that has already shot up fast, is **chasing the market,** which usually leads to the unwanted situation of riding the stock down.

One school of Wall Streeters prefers to go **bottom fishing,** looking for stocks that have had a poor showing recently. These players adopt the market maxim, "Buy a straw hat in winter," buying a stock when no one else wants it on the assumption that soon the unwanted item will be in as much demand as a straw hat in summer.

Bottom fishers searching for cheap stock may be **trading on a shoestring** (an old market expression possibly borrowed from the game of faro), which means trading with little money, usually on margin. Margin trading entails putting down a percentage of the purchase price and borrowing the rest with interest from the brokerage. In the old days, if the small investment grew into a sizable profit, they said that the speculator had "run a shoestring up to a tannery" or "started on a shoestring and run it up to a tannery."

A speculator on a shoestring can try to stretch the small amount of money by **pyramiding,** particularly in commodities where margin requirements are low. (Pyramids can be built in **short** positions, explained below.) In building a pyramid, after an initial investment that succeeds, the speculator uses the paper profits as margin to increase the size of the position. If the price keeps going up, the investor can continue on the dangerous path of pyramiding. But if the price falls before the paper profits are turned into cash, the pyramid collapses and the whole investment disappears.

The **bubble,** another notorious market structure based on buying, has been luring gullible speculators for many years, in Europe and the United States. Like pyramids, bubbles rest on the shaky foundation of investors' hopes, not on sound business practices. When speculators finally realize that the company has nothing to offer, the bubble bursts. The apt term "bubble" comes from seventeenth-century slang for cheating, as in the 1609 phrase, "To bubble you out of a sum of money."

The most famous two bubbles, the South Sea Bubble and the Mississippi Bubble, took their names from the financially hollow **bubble companies** that had lured in the public in France and England. Their disastrous collapses in the 1720s prompted the British government to pass the **bubble acts,** aimed at preventing such illusory schemes.

A "Reformed Stock Gambler" who wrote *Stocks and Stock-Jobbing in Wall Street* in 1848 explained that bubbles cast their spells on this side of the Atlantic, too. In a section titled "Inflations and Explosions," the writer extended the metaphor:

> The beautiful bubbles manufactured in Wall Street, whose varying hues of transcendent brilliancy as they are wafted along by prosperous gales, tempt an admiring public to grasp at them, and—get "sucked in" by their mysterious disappearance.

A trader can create a small bubble in a stock through the illegal practice of *goosing the market*. A *goose job* consists of forcing up the price by buying outstanding shares at increasing prices, thus creating demand for the stock. In 1987, when the Japanese bought American stocks in massive amounts, critics complained they were *goosing the bowl*, raising prices overall, although not with the illegal intent of a goose job.

HOLDING ON

The conservative investor, who avoids pyramids, bubbles, and traders goosing the market, favors instead buying solid stocks and *salting them down*, that is, holding on to them. These investors follow the Wall Street saying "Buy 'em and put 'em away." As a writer in 1871 explained,

> When an operator has been lucky, withdraws his gains from the hazard of the street, and invests in good dividend paying stock, he is said to have salted down his money.[2]

"Invest in a stock that will let you sleep" offers similar advice, expanded in a story told by Dickson G. Watts, president from 1878 to 1880 of the wild New York Cotton Exchange.

> A man was so nervous that a friend asked him what was the matter. "I can't sleep," he explained. "Why not?" asked the friend. "I am carrying so much cotton that I lay awake nights

thinking about it. What can I do?" "Sell it down to the sleeping point," answered the friend.

Worried investors might find that **hedging** eases their sleep. A financial term since the 1600s, and listed in stock market dictionaries since 1900, **to hedge** means to balance out positions, with an eye to minimizing possible losses. Options provide a popular instrument for hedging against drops in stock, while the futures market allows farmers and other commodity owners to protect themselves against a fall in prices.

Certain market situations make it impossible to sell (or buy) a stock, even if an investor wants to. For example, if a specialist on the Exchange floor cannot handle the volume of orders in a stock, the Exchange **shuts the stock down,** temporarily suspending trading in it until the problem is solved.

Individually, investors may find themselves **locked-in** to a stock, holding it because if they sold immediately, the large profit would be subject to capital gains tax; or because the sale would mean a large loss. The fact that someone in this predicament could sell, but chooses not to, prompted a writer in 1969 to describe **locked-in** as "A stupid phrase meaning unable to sell because the person has (a) too large a loss, or (b) too large a gain, or (c) too small a brain."[3]

A **frozen account** also prevents an investor from trading, at least temporarily. This occurs when the investor has a history of late payment for stocks or of selling stocks before they are paid for. The NYSE takes a dim view of such behavior and punishes repeat offenders by requiring that their accounts be frozen for ninety days. During that period, the customer must pay in full when buying a stock and must deliver the stock before selling.

When Wall Streeters choose to hold stocks because the market makes them nervous, they are **pulling in their horns.** Bulls with long positions stop buying, and bears who have gone short call a halt to it. As an old market adage, sometimes called the golden rule of trading, advocates, "When in doubt, do nothing."

WHEN THE SHIP STARTS TO SINK

In a variation on trading's golden rule, they also say on the Street, "When in doubt, get out." Similar advice is echoed in the well-known proverb, "Your first loss is your best loss," which recommends selling as soon as the price starts to drop, not waiting until losses mount up. However, if the decline turns out to be temporary and the stock goes back up, the investor who sold in haste has lost potential profits and paid a commission, which explains a contrasting Wall street proverb, "The easiest way to go broke is being right too soon." But most Street wisdom comes down on the side of caution—when market great Bernard Baruch was once asked, "How did you make so much money?" he replied, "By selling too soon."

Yet another old piece of market wisdom tells investors, "Run quickly or not at all," meaning to sell at the first sign of danger or, failing that, hold on to the stock until the storm has died down. A customer who has decided to run quickly tells her broker *to hit the bid,* a market order to sell at the bid price—the highest current offer—rather than negotiate for a higher price. In a more casual manner, the customer could say *blow it off* or *blow out the position,* that is, sell the stock immediately. Similarly, an unethical broker who has made a trade for a customer just for the sake of the commission has *blown the customer out after a point* (a point means a dollar) or *played him for a point.*

In formal English, a Wall Streeter might say that when stocks are sold and converted to cash, the speculator has liquidated the account—one of the many terms on the market concerning liquid. Slang supplies numerous synonyms for liquidating, several of which express a sense of hurry.

If prices begin dropping and droves of investors hurry to sell, afraid they will be caught in a falling market, Wall Streeters say they are *running for the hills.* They are hoping to escape the flood that comes when everyone liquidates. They are *bailing out,* selling quickly without regard to price, also called *unloading.* A 1911 writer commented:

It is sometimes said that the person who "unloaded" succeeded in "getting ashore." This is a bit of slang, which suggests a person getting ashore from a sinking boat in season to prevent drowning.[4]

Unloading, dumping, and *spilling* all mean selling large amounts of stock at once. Typically this happens when the speculator realizes that the price is falling, but sometimes he dumps the stock for the purpose of lowering the price, an illegal action in today's market. The culprit *saddles the market* with numerous shares, letting the principle of supply and demand drive the price down. Early in this century, when groups of speculators purposely lowered prices this way, Wall Streeters called it *hammering the stock* or *pounding;* in England at the same time, traders termed it *banging the market,* and those who did it were *bangers,* words sometimes used on this side of the Atlantic.

A pattern in selling too late, *distress selling,* occurs when the market falls and those who have bought on margin receive a margin *call,* requiring more money to maintain their accounts. If they don't answer the call, the brokerages convert the accounts to cash in *distress sales.* One ill-timed understatement that preceded the market crash in 1929 came from J. P. Morgan partner Thomas Lamont, who was quoted as saying on October 24, "There has been a little distress selling on the Stock Exchange."

SHORT SELLING AND SHORT SQUEEZING

The market technique of *going short* mystifies many outsiders, and even baffles some investors who take long positions, but who view going short as the realm of professionals. *Short selling,* an expression in use since 1852, occurs when a speculator sells a stock he doesn't own but which he has borrowed from his brokerage. The *short seller* hopes the price will fall so that he can buy the stock (to return to the brokerage) at the lower price, having sold it at a higher one, and so make a profit. The short sellers as a group make up the *short interest,* a phrase that also describes the total number of NYSE shares that are currently sold short. Bears take *short positions,* and bulls take long ones.

Because the short seller profits only if the stock's price goes down, and because many more investors go long than go short, general sentiment goes against short sellers. The much-quoted admonition "Don't sell America short," attributed to the elder J. P. Morgan, condemns bears as unpatriotic. In answer to this, a famous floor trader in the 1920s, who knew how profitable short selling could be, liked to tell his junior colleagues, "This is a great country, but my advice to you is to forget that fact once in a while."[5]

Short sellers defend their practice by observing that they cushion the market when prices are falling. Except by illegal manipulations, bears don't cause the market to fall, even if they profit when it does. Nevertheless, the expression *sell short* has come to mean "to disparage, to betray" in general slang.

When short sellers buy stocks to fulfill the obligations from short selling, they are *covering their shorts.* If the price of the stock goes up instead of down and appears to be going even higher, the speculator tries to buy the stock quickly, *running to cover.* A prank at Amex made fun of such a plight:

> On a rally following a market drop, those who had been selling short might find their underwear yanked out above their trousers. ("Getting the shorts by the shorts.")[6]

During market manipulations, powerful speculators may purposely try to raise the price of a stock that many have sold short. By raising the price suddenly and sharply, the bulls compel the bears, who are *caught short,* into covering their shorts at a loss to avoid an even larger loss in the future. Around the turn of the century, Wall Streeters called the manipulation *twisting the shorts,* defined by one writer as "putting on the screws."

In the most extreme form of manipulation, when the bulls have purposely *cornered the market* in a stock by buying up all available shares, they *squeeze the shorts* in a *short-squeeze play,* forcing them to buy at artificially high prices, to the great profit of the manipulators. When the bulls ruthlessly twisted those who had taken short positions in Harlem Railroad during 1865, the event went down in history as the **Harlem Squeeze.** Similar manipulations, although currently illegal, still occur now and then.

The dangers of selling short keep many small investors from trying it, and even experienced short sellers still quote, if somewhat jokingly, the warning attributed to Daniel Drew, the Great Bear:

> *He who sells what isn't his'n*
> *Must buy it back or go to pris'n.*

Short selling presents no dangers in the variation which Wall Street lingo calls **selling against the box, going short against the box** or **boxing.** In this transaction, used for tax purposes, the investor does own the stock in question, but hopes to buy more at a lower price to cover the short sale, rather than using the shares already salted away. The slang term box arose from the practice of investors keeping their stock certificates in safety deposit boxes; with the advent of computers, the practice has largely died out, but the old expression lingers on.

WIPED OUT, TIPPED OUT, AND BLOWN OUT

His losses were terrible. He is now poor. He has no money, no stock, and is of no account in the market. In the langauge of the street, he is "wiped out."[7]

Thus Matthew Hale Smith described a young man whose trading techniques had backfired in 1871. **Wiped out,** still a popular phrase, can mean more specifically that a broker has closed an investor's margin account because the margin money was exhausted. Today Wall Streeters also say the speculator was **tapped out,** and if complete loss follows, it's **tap city** for him. Since trading on margin presents more dangers for investors than buying stocks outright, margin investors more often **tip out** or get *blown out,* that is, lose everything they invested and still owe money.

Wall Street shares with the rest of the country slang phrases indicating large losses, phrases heard so often among market players that they are listed in stock market dictionaries. For example, *taking a bath* and *taking a cleaning* are included in a 1975 glossary, both explained as "sustaining serious losses in investments." The definition for *taking a bath* goes on,

> It is also expressed as being taken to the cleaners, wiped out and being murdered on Wall Street. When a stock suffers a sudden and serious decline in market price, perhaps 50%, 75% or even more in decline, it is said to fall out of bed, while the owners of the stock take a bath as a result.[8]

Yet another stock market synonym for taking a bath is *going through the financial wringer,* which refers to an apparatus for squeezing the water out of laundry. The market phrase is a variation on the general slang of "going through the wringer," going through an experience that causes pain or hardship. The recurring imagery of becoming cleaner when one loses money crops up again in the expression *cleaned out,* meaning that an investor has lost all his money, as if his pockets had been emptied. An investor may also *take some gas, go to the wall, be burned,* or find his investments have *gone south,* all of which indicate losses.

When a specialist on the exchange floor has to buy undesirable stock in order to maintain an orderly market in it, he complains about having to *eat the stock.* Similarly, an investor who ends up owning stocks that are no longer desirable is *holding the bag,* a market expression used since at least 1903. (*Holding the baby,* on the other hand, has been defined in Street slang as holding a stock in hopes of future profit.) When knowledgeable Wall Streeters sell a stock at an opportune time, they leave behind them *bagholders,* those less sophisticated speculators who still own the stock as its price drops. Joe Granville, who writes an influential market letter, sings a song called "Bagholder Blues" at his seminars, poking fun at naive investors. But professionals also get *bagged,* for example, when a trader has a trade stolen from him on the floor. If a dealer buys a large amount of a stock from an institution that is secretly unloading more of the same stock elsewhere, the institution has bagged the dealer. Deceiving dealers often gives the institution a reputation for **bagging the Street.**

MAKING A KILLING LEAVES YOU STANDING ON VELVET

Perhaps because making money speaks for itself, or because people make money less often than they lose it, Wall Streeters have fewer slang expressions for doing well than for doing badly. The slang they do have is shared by the general public, who also use the phrases **to make a killing** and **to clean up.** Both slang expressions appear in Frank Norris's 1902 novel *The Pit:* "Here's your chance to make a killing," one character advises another; later in the book a market manipulator announces, "We pulled it off, and I've cleaned up five hundred thousand dollars."[9]

Less frequently heard is the old-fashioned phrase **standing on velvet,** a phrase borrowed from the British, that used to be popular among gamblers as well as speculators. Language expert J. L. Dillard writes about it,

> If [a] player who starts with very little is lucky, in faro or in business, he can wind up *on velvet. Velvet* was the faro term for money won from the house. By 1901, Westerners were using the term for 'profit or gain beyond what is usual or expected'.[10]

SELL ON THE BLIPS

The job of trading—on the exchange floors, in firm trading rooms, or over the counter—employs a language of its own. A novice listening to traders will have trouble understanding the words—partly because traders talk so fast, and partly because they rely so heavily on slang and jargon.

In their everyday speech, Wall Street traders drop the "dollars" in naming a price, so that they say a stock that is selling at twenty dollars a share is selling "at twenty." Keeping this in mind, an outsider can interpret the advice that made the rounds in the options pits in the mid-1970s when IBM was selling between 240 and 280; just before the stock split, a popular couplet urged traders to "Sell the 280s, buy a Mercedes."

The shorthand for prices also provides the basis for a common Wall Street joke, which has many versions including one from 1983 about herpes and Whoopies given earlier, and this one from around 1929:

> One broker says to another, "How come you look so glum to-day?" and the other replies, "You'd look glum too if you had arteriosclerosis at forty-five." "That's nothing," counters the first broker, "I had Internal Combustion at 103."

Because stock prices move in eighths, traders give the fractions slang names: a *quack* for a quarter, a *laugh* for a half, *fried eggs* for five-eighths, and *all the eighths* for seven-eighths. Where price varies by one-sixteenth, the fraction is shortened to *teenie.*

In bond trading, the bonds go up and down in *nickels* or *dimes,* five basis points (.05%) or ten (.10%) in the yield of the security. Even in casual conversation in the inflated world of trading, a nickel can mean much more than five cents, as a newcomer at the Merc found out the dangerous way. The story goes that she bet "a nickel" on the outcome of the Super Bowl, only to find out after the game ended that she had waged—and luckily, won— five thousand dollars.

Wall Streeters say that stock prices move in *ticks.* Derived from the ticker tape days, tick used to mean a transaction that appeared on the tape; now it refers to which direction the price moves in a trade. A tape-watcher tracking every move of a stock follows it *tick-by-tick,* making note of every *uptick,* which indicates that the most recent transaction in the stock took place at a higher price than the previous one, and every *downtick* at a lower price. The *uptick rule* in Wall Street lingo refers to the SEC requirement that short sales be made at one-eighth of a point or more above the preceding sale, *on the uptick.*

Traders also call an uptick, a *plus-tick,* and the uptick rule, the *plus-tick rule.* As a gag, workers on the NYSE floor will send a novice to find a "box of plus-ticks," as if they were sticks of some kind.

When the market as a whole moves up slightly, the minor trend may be dubbed an *uptick. Blip* means a minor fluctuation either way in the market, though some Wall Streeters confine it to a movement upward, as in the maxim "Buy on the dips, sell on the blips," a newer version of "Buy on weakness, sell on strength."

When a stock price plummets, suffering more than just a downtick, traders are apt to say, "It's *glove sizes* for that one." As one San Francisco broker explained it, "Suits are sized in the thirties and forties, shirts in the teens, hats around seven and gloves around three or four, directly corresponding to points on the Stock Exchange."

WHEN THE ELEPHANTS BUY

The most powerful animals today in the Wall Street menagerie are *elephants,* as institutional investors are sometimes called. In the past few decades, pension funds, mutual funds, and similar big institutions have come to account for eighty to ninety percent of stock exchange trading, in large transactions called *block trades,* and their trading habits have given rise to an array of slang terms.

For example, in a *cross,* a broker deals with an institutional investor who wants to sell a large block of stock, and another client who wants to buy just that block. The transaction is made on the exchange floor, with the permission of the specialist, in such a way that the broker gets both commissions. When the stock is so easily crossed, Wall Streeters scoff at the transaction as a *no-brainer,* which can also mean a stock that a broker recommends to clients based on a list from the firm's research department.

In a new variation in block trades, dubbed *sunshine trading,* the trader announces ahead of time plans to execute a large order, typically a block of futures contracts. Advocates of the *sunshine trade,* which dispenses with the secrecy that typically precedes sale of a large block, claim that more information creates a more efficient market, an explanation that has not persuaded many to try it.

The *give-up,* in which one brokerage firm shared its commission on a transaction with another, grew in popularity when mutual funds burgeoned in the 1960s. The mutual funds started exploiting the give-up, a practice and word dating back to 1903, as a way to reward brokers for selling mutual-fund shares to the public. In 1968, the SEC outlawed give-ups, which critics likened to kickbacks, and established a volume discount—promptly dubbed *V.D.*—for trades of more than 1,000 shares.

The portfolio managers who run Wall Street's elephants feel intense pressure to perform well, pressure that sometimes drives them to become *closet indexers.* Instead of picking stocks themselves, they secretly model their investments after a stock market index, such as the Standard & Poor's 500. Thus, they are guaranteed to do no worse than a respectable market average, although they're certain to lose the respect of colleagues who suspect them of the ploy.

In another scheme for looking good, money managers at institutional funds *dress up their portfolios* by selling unsuccessful stocks and buying showier ones at the end of each quarter, when their performance is about to be judged. With this *window dressing,* the manager hopes to satisfy current customers and—as the window dresser at a department store does—lure in new customers with the eye-catching display.

As a way to make a portfolio look more conservative, its manager may take a *flight to quality,* in which he wings his way from lower-rated to higher-rated bonds, or, less frequently, from speculative to blue-chip stocks. Wall Streeters call the replacement of a poorer-quality security with a higher-quality one *trading up,* an expression now infiltrating general slang. "Just the other day,"

wrote a *New York Times* columnist, "I heard a woman, referring
to her second marriage, announce that she had 'traded up.' "

The Tip

A *tip is very quiet,*
It doesn't make much noise;
But what a sacred thing it is
Among the Wall Street boys.

It tells you just what stocks and bonds
Are going up and why;
It fills you with the impulse
To immediately buy.[11]

So go two verses in "The Tip," from a 1926 collection of poems
titled *Stock Market Quotations.* Then as now, many an investor
succumbed to a *tip* in deciding what to buy, what to sell, and
what to hold. A tip, once also known as a *pointer,* conveys information, said to be confidential, about how a security or commodity will move. *Tipsters* whisper their quiet news to *tippees,* who
may pass it on to *subtippees,* as the SEC calls the secondary
recipients of inside information. A skeptical tippee may *copper a*
tip, defined by stock market glossaries from the first half of this
century as "to do just the opposite of what you are advised."

For years, tipsters have been spreading their news far and wide
to customers who subscribe to *tipster sheets,* newsletters that offer
market forecasts and often push certain stocks. For just as many
years, dissatisfied readers have been complaining about the worth-
lessness of the *tout sheets,* as they're also called. In 1919, for
example, the anonymous author of *P.S. What Do You Think of*
the Market? waxed sarcastic about a newsletter writer:

He always says that if the market don't go up maybe it should
go down and if it rains next Tuesday the sidewalks will be wet.[12]

Although many market letters provide legitimate information,
others *puff* stocks—as it's been called for more than a hundred
years—that is, praise them knowing the stocks are losers. These

tipster sheets run *zingers,* paid stock promotions disguised as unbiased reports, in an illegal scheme that allows the newsletter writer and his colleagues to buy stock first, then sell it after the newsletter comes out and drives up the price.

FRIVOLOUS FORECASTING

While tips give doubtful guidance on specific stocks, Wall Streeters turn in a joking fashion to certain market indicators for equally doubtful advice on the market as a whole. The range of theories to predict the market reveals Wall Street's vivid imagination. For example, one says that if the color yellow rises in popularity in fashion and decorating, the market will rise, and if yellow falls out of fashion, stocks will fall. Another contends that, in men's clothing, wider ties signal a falling market, narrow ties a rising one. Other Wall Streeters put their faith in the batting averages of professional baseball players, or snow on the ground in Boston on Christmas Day. But the two most prevalent theories hinge on women's hemlines and on the Super Bowl football game.

Everyone in the market has heard at one time or another about the *hemline theory,* attributed to Ralph Rotnem who worked at Harris, Upham. It holds that markets follow the length of hems on women's dresses. The higher the hem, the higher the market will go, and the lower the hem, the lower the market. The juxtaposition of the miniskirt and the soaring market during the sixties bolstered this theory.

Linking women's clothes and the stock market as early as 1910, a column in *Moody's Magazine* that year explained that some Wall Streeters blamed women's clothing for market problems. The writer, in discussing why the current market was in a slump, blamed the government, with the "flimflams of the Jim Keenes" and "the wide prevalence of 'New Yorkitis' " as contributing factors. He added,

> There is a wild acclaim from some quarters that it is the extravagance of the women, the cost of women's hats and gowns, which has brought on the slump in stocks.[13]

In January, Wall Streeters turn their attention to the Super Bowl as a market indicator. They predict that if a team that was a member of the original National Football League wins the Super Bowl, the market will go up that year. If a team from the Old American League wins, the market will go down. Advocates of the theory point out, tongue-in-cheek, that it has an excellent track record for predicting the upcoming market year. They add that Wall Streeters who believe they know which way the market will go can use the theory in placing their bets on the game.

The joking tone of these theories acknowledges that, despite the many efforts to predict it, the market remains unpredictable. The frivolous forecasting serves to relieve tension, for, as a Wall Street rhyme conveys, every aspect of trading can bring about anxiety:

> *Buy and you'll be sorry*
> *Sell and you'll regret*
> *Hold and you will worry*
> *Do nothing and you'll fret.*

6

The Fantasy World of Corporate Takeovers

In the last ten years, the wave of hostile corporate takeovers has spawned a host of new words in the Wall Street lexicon. So strange and colorful is this new slang that members of the public who encounter it don't know what to think. When Pennzoil took Texaco to court in 1985 over Texaco's controversial acquisition of Getty Oil, jurors had difficulty understanding the takeover slang terms used by Barton Winokur, witness for Getty. According to *The Wall Street Journal*, "His habit of slipping into jargon only aroused the suspicions of Texas jurors over the ethics of the takeover business," so lawyers had him define terms for the jury including **bear hug, in play,** and **shark.**[1]

The new slang terms taken together draw a picture of danger and romance that transforms the business world into a battlefield and a marriage chamber. Some Wall Streeters complain that the romantic, violent, sometimes humorous slang misleads the public into seeing takeovers as a self-indulgent waste of time and resources. But if these Wall Streeters are right, they have to blame their colleagues, who invented words and phrases so catchy that they inevitably draw publicity.

ROMANCE, RAPE, AND SHOTGUN MARRIAGE

When Wall Streeters speak of corporate mergers, they use sexual metaphors, from marriage to rape. For example, in a merger agreeable to both parties, a *suitor* makes a bid for the target, sometimes with the help of a *corporate marriage broker,* an investment banker or other financial adviser who collects a large fee if the merger works out. If extensive friendly negotiations for a merger fail, the result is *sex without marriage.* A successful venture ends with the the two companies *brought to the altar* and the merger consummated.

In a situation neither friendly nor unfriendly, a company may receive a *bisexual offer* about which the target's board of directors expresses—of all things—neutrality. As the prospective buyer raises the price and assures executives job security, the target gets friendlier and the offer may result in corporate marriage.

At one time, no prestigious corporation or "gentleman" would have bought another company without its cooperation. Only disreputable upstarts, called *raiders,* bought companies against the will of management. But then came a wave of unfriendly takeovers by respectable corporations whom Wall Street dubbed *blue-chip raiders.* Because stock prices had fallen, acquiring a company looked better than financing new plants, and the motto of these new raiders was "It's cheaper to buy than to build." In the first *blue-chip raid,* the highly regarded investment bank of Morgan Stanley aided International Nickel in the 1974 hostile takeover of ESB Inc. Investment bankers call it the first tender offer of a new era, a turning point in takeover history (and slang).

Before the blue-chip raiders joined the fray, most observers believed that unfriendly acquirers cared little about the future of a target company. They were out to "milk it" of its assets and leave the shareholders with an "empty shell." Critics of hostile takeovers characterized this as "rape," pointing out that employees often lost their jobs due to cutbacks or plant shutdowns. Now that the quality of raiders has changed, more financial experts rise to their defense, saying the raids keep otherwise fat and complacent managements on their toes and ensure that shareholders get the true value of their investments. But those who lose in the battle still call it rape.

One alternative to hostile takeover is finding a more congenial buyer—once called an *angel* or *sweetheart,* now called a *white knight*—to outbid the raider. But even if such a marriage can be arranged, rarely do the two parties live happily ever after. White knights, who must decide under pressure and cannot always study the target carefully, may find out too late that the company they rescued is not as enticing as it first appeared. As for the rescued company, Wall Street speaks of its fate as a "shotgun marriage," where the raider is holding a gun to the target's head (though the metaphor switches the usual male and female roles). The company loses its independence, which means its executives lose power and sometimes their jobs when the white knight moves in.

A spirit of machismo dominates the takeover scene, as seen in the images of aggression and sexual conquest. Wall Streeters say jokingly that doing a hostile deal is like sex—you don't know what it's like until you've tried it. Male companies conquer female companies, often fighting off other males in the process. Hostile takeovers are tests of manliness (few women take part in them) in which raiders prove their prowess by empire building and targets prove theirs, if they are lucky, by remaining independent. Critics complain that raiders are motivated more by the need to feed their egos than by the financial merits of acquisitions.

Wickedness and daring—useful traits for empire-building—appear in the slang for acquirers: *raiders, black knights, pirates,* and *buccaneers.* Drawn from legends and adventure stories, these descriptions add an aura of fantasy to the takeover scene. Defenders of hostile raids complain that the pejorative terms prejudice the public against the idea of takeovers. But to others, the language sounds romantic, conjuring up a picture of daredevil swashbucklers out to find fame and fortune.

The fortune they are seeking, as told in slang, often takes the form of a woman. One common slang name for the target company, *sleeping beauty,* comes from the familiar fairy tale (more fantasy material) in which a young princess sleeps for a hundred years—the archetypal passive female. Stories of her beauty attract many would-be suitors who cannot get past the briars on the castle, until one prince succeeds and awakens her with a kiss. (In some versions, he succeeds not through bravery but through perfect timing—the curse of sleep and the deadliness of the briars expire after exactly one hundred years, just as he arrives.)

The corporate sleeping beauty, sometimes called the *maiden,* attracts admirers with the cash on its balance sheet and its undervalued, sleeper stock. When the takeover wars had just begun, raids caught many such slumbering targets by surprise. They were oblivious to the outside interest they excited, and were asleep on the job, at least according to raiders who claim that typically the target company's management had failed to exploit the company's potential. For example, when Saul Steinberg raided Walt Disney Productions, the unexploited potential consisted of two neglected aspects of Disney, its Florida real estate holdings and its library of old films. The chairman of the sleeping beauty admitted about Steinberg's attack, "It woke us up."

The slang reveals that to be in a position of lesser power in the takeover wars is equivalent to being female—the pursuer is male, the acquired, female. When the protesting target company cries for help, Wall Street again gives it a female name, *damsel in distress* (although some limit this label to money-losing corporations "well endowed with enormous tax-loss carry-forwards which are attractive to acquiring companies that can take advantage of them").

In a 1981 novel by Alexandra Marshall titled *Tender Offer,* the female head of a target elaborates on the sexual implications of takeovers as she explains the position of her company, Phoebe's Fudge, to a friend:

> "I was told this morning that I ought to count on a merger of some kind, even if we succeed over Syncorp. We're much too ripe and irresistible, I'm told, not to belong to someone."[2]

It is in keeping with these sex roles that the damsel seeks rescue from a (male) *white knight,* who becomes the opponent of the raider. The term white knight, part of the financial lexicon since at least 1977, gained popularity due to its inclusion in Martin Lipton's 1978 book *Takeovers and Freezeouts,* as did other terms including black knight and bear hug. White knight comes from general slang for "a champion of good causes." But unlike King Arthur's knights, who sought chivalrous deeds to perform, corporate white knights do not act out of gallantry. The damsel must be as "ripe and irresistible" to the rescuer as she is to the raider. The more undervalued the target, the more attractive it is to both. The larger the target, the harder it is to find a savior.

If relations between the damsel and her would-be rescuer cool, the white knight may become a *gray knight* who still pursues the target but is no longer welcome. This souring of the engagement may cause the target company to accept the original raider's offer. Gray knight also refers to a second bidder who was not solicited by the target company, but who tries to take advantage of its difficulties.

When Martin Marietta was fighting off the Bendix Corporation in 1982, it solicited the support of Harry J. Gray of United Technologies, not to enter as a white knight but to help Martin Marietta buy Bendix in a counterattack. In this fray, punsters dubbed him the *Gray Knight* in his role of a fellow predator hoping to split the spoils of battle. Harry Gray, an experienced *takeover artist,* has played every role in the melodrama: friendly suitor, white knight, gray knight, and raider. In the last of these personas he has been nicknamed the *Gray Acquisitor* and the *Gray Shark.* Because he often traveled by helicopter, executives who worried that he might prey on their company joked dryly that they could hear the whirring blades overhead.

Once a company has been approached by one raider, "the blood is in the water," as Wall Street puts it, and sharks gather around for the kill. *Sharks,* sometimes called *Wall Street piranhas,* are purchasers eager to take advantage of a wounded target. According to the conventional wisdom, only one company in five remains independent after a bid has been made, even if it succeeds in resisting the first offer. Any raid with its concomitant publicity puts the target *in play* or *into play,* and turns the eyes of the financial community toward it.

Among those on the look-out for companies about to go into play are the risk arbitrageurs, stock market professionals who buy huge quantities of a suspected target's stock in expectation that the final tender offer will be at a higher price. Because these *arbs* have no loyalty to the companies whose stock they own, they prove useful to the raiders as short-term speculators looking for the quick profit. They are said to "swim with the sharks," feeding off the wounded target.

The arbs focus their sharp-sighted eyes on the large brokerage houses looking for signs of a raid, while outside investors and smaller arbs fix their attention on the top arbs. Consequently, brokerages and important arbs have taken to disguising their trades. As one colleague explained about Ivan Boesky, the most closely watched of the arbitrageurs, "He likes a beard when he trades." The image of wearing a beard as a disguise has led to the slang word *beard,* to describe a broker at one of the smaller brokerage houses who buys up stock in relative secrecy for bidders and arbs who want to hide their intentions. One expert at *bearding,* Ace Greenberg of Bear Stearns, received a camouflage suit from fellow traders after he helped T. Boone Pickens acquire 9 percent of Gulf Oil without stirring up interest.

THE ATTACK: BEAR HUGS AND BLITZKREIGS

Cloak-and-dagger secrecy characterizes several aspects of the takeover attacks. In spy-novel fashion, when raiders or research teams investigate potential targets, they customarily conceal the identity of targets by using code names, a practice that brings out the poetic on Wall Street. Early names verify the sexual and aggressive nature of raids. In Leasco's takeover of Reliance, the raider called the target *Raquel,* from the sexy movie star Raquel Welch, to describe Reliance's financial voluptuousness. In another take-

over plan, Leasco nicknamed Chemical Bank *Faye,* after Faye
Dunaway's role as a bank robber in the movie *Bonnie and Clyde.*

The Salomon Brothers research team working for Bendix christened Bendix *Earth,* Martin Marietta *Fire,* and RCA *Wind,* using three of the four basic elements, or perhaps naming them
from the soul group Earth, Wind and Fire. In an operation dubbed
Mazel Tov, Hebrew for "good luck" or "congratulations," American Express, calling itself *Tiger,* pursued Trade Development
Bank, called *Copper.* In a 1985 raid on Revlon by Pantry Pride,
the code name *Nicole* (for Revlon) came from the name of a
seventeen-month-old girl, the daughter of one of the lawyers.

Secrecy is most important in the method of attack called the
creeping tender or *creeping control campaign* in which an unfriendly suitor secretly amasses a growing block of the target company's stock. Buying quietly keeps the price down. Before showing his hand, the pursuer acquires a *toehold purchase,* just below
the SEC limit at which a purchase must be made public. Even
if the takeover does not succeed, the stock price usually rises once
the target is in play, and, having bought low, the raider can cash
in his chips at a profit. (Or the target may resort to *greenmail,*
explained later.) Victims of the creeping tender describe it as a
"slow death," more painful than an outright declaration of war.

Before making a public offer, a suitor may approach the target
with a *teddy-bear pat,* a letter or telephone call that indicates the
suitor is prepared to make a bid. Because this approach does not
mention a specific price, the target does not need to make a public announcement and both sides can avoid publicity. The teddy-
bear pat, also called a *casual pass,* leaves open the possibility of a
friendly merger, or a graceful withdrawal if the suitor chooses not
to pursue an unwilling target.

If the target rebuffs the pass, and the suitor wants to persist, he
may make an official *tender offer,* a publicly made invitation to
all shareholders to tender their shares for sale at a given price.
Although *tender* in this context means "to offer for sale," writers
cannot resist wordplay on its other meaning of "loving and solic-
itous." In the novel *Tender Offer,* mentioned earlier, two plots

develop side by side: the tender offer for the fudge company and the romance between the female executive and her ardent suitor. The book leaves the reader uncertain about the company's fate, closing instead with the executive becoming happily engaged to be married. In the business of takeovers the endings tend to be less blissful, for, in the words of one executive whose company was attacked, "The colorful language is about the only thing 'tender' about a tender offer." Those attacked refer to tender offers, often sprung on them by surprise, as **tender traps.**

The trap may be a two-step one, sometimes described as **double-barreled.** In a **two-step tender** or a **two-tiered tender,** the aggressor makes an initial offer of cash for the target's stock to gain a controlling interest, then makes a second offer for the rest at a lower price, usually with some form of security. Described as **front-loaded,** this arrangement benefits those who tender their shares quickly.

In the first years of the current takeover wave, raiders delighted in the **blitzkreig tender offer,** which hit the target hard and fast. *Blitzkreig*, German for "lightning war," means a war conducted with great speed and force and, appropriate to the takeover imagery of male and female, soldiers used *blitzkreig* during World War II to mean "a quick line used to gain sympathy from an attractive girl."

An infamous version of the blitzkreig tender offer was the **Saturday Night Special,** an unexpected takeover bid aimed at achieving control before the target's management could muster resistance. Raiders would make their surprise bid over the weekend, on Friday afternoon or Saturday evening, catching the target offguard when the stock market was closed.

In the case that gave the maneuver its name, Colt Industries announced a bid for the shares of a smaller firm, Garlock, in November 1975. The offer was due to expire in eight days, under the regulations at that time, giving Garlock little time to fight back. Garlock thought it had found a white knight in AMF, but the two companies had a falling out that transformed AMF into a gray knight and prompted Garlock to go with Colt's offer.

One of Garlock's public relations advisers, Richard Cheney of Hill & Knowlton, coined the term *Saturday Night Special,* playing on the fact that Colt manufactures guns. Cheney was purposely denigrating Colt's bid for Garlock, implying that the offer was "cheap and that it went off quickly" by equating it with a small, cheap handgun nicknamed the Saturday Night Special. State legislatures have put a halt to corporate Saturday Night Specials by lengthening the minimum number of days between a tender offer announcement and its expiration, thus eliminating the pressure to act within a week.

Another gun in the slang of takeover wars is the *smoking gun,* a mistake made by the raider, such as violating a federal regulation, that gives the target extra time for defense. The phrase comes from general slang, best known from Watergate, in which *smoking gun* means a piece of indisputable evidence, especially of a crime; it is derived from the detective-novel stereotype of a person standing at the scene of a murder holding a recently fired, still smoking gun.

When the Saturday Night Special lost its bite, the *bear hug,* an escalation of the teddy-bear pat, became a popular method of attack. Another play on words, the phrase bear hug brings to mind a congenial exchange between two friends. The corporate hug also appears mild at first, starting off with a letter from a prospective suitor to a target company. But a closer look shows that the bear hug is more like the attack of a bear than the greeting of a friend, for the letter writer intends to squeeze the target into accepting. The letter, addressed to the directors, specifies a price and reminds the directors that they have a fiduciary responsibility to their shareholders to accept a good bid. When the technique was first used, directors felt they had to make the letter public, which backed them into a corner. The raider who wanted to give a *strong bear hug* made a public announcement to tighten the squeeze as soon as the letter went out. But the bear hug strategy lost strength when the courts indicated that fiduciary responsibility did not require the directors to accept a bid as long as they considered the offer in "good faith."

(The ludicrousness of hugging in the context of corporate mergers provides the humor in a 1985 *New Yorker* cartoon by James Stevenson in which one smiling businessman with his arms outstretched is saying to another, disgruntled businessman, "Now that the merger is completed, Stahlmeyer, how's about a hug?")

Corporations dread takeovers in part because successful raiders often dismantle their new possession. They sell off subsidiaries, they say, to streamline the company, but old management sees it as sheer greed. In **bootstrap bust-ups**—another phrase attributed to Martin Lipton—the takeovers are financed by borrowing with the intention of paying the debt by selling assets, "busting up" the corporation. "Bootstrap," like shoestring, implies a lack of funds. Practitioners of this strategy, such as T. Boone Pickens and Carl Icahn, are known as **bust-up artists.**

The investment bankers who aid the bust-up artists become the targets of corporate hatred, hence a joke that made the rounds in 1987:

> How many investment bankers does it take to change a light bulb?
>
> Two. One to smash the bulb with a baseball bat and one to find buyers for the fragments.

SHARK REPELLENTS AND OTHER DEFENSIVE MOVES

Once the takeover wars expanded, sleeping beauties awoke to their danger and learned to shore up their defenses before raiders appeared, with an aim to making the company **bulletproof.** Typically they begin by putting on retainer teams of lawyers, investment bankers, and public relations experts who, like the similar teams employed by raiders, are known as **hired guns.** Another nickname for them is **killer bees.** Another early step has been the compiling of a **black book,** kept under lock and key, that spells out a battle plan with step-by-step directions of how to respond to a tender offer. Like the bachelor's "little black book," it lists names and addresses, in this case, of managers, directors, and outside advisers rather than eligible women. However, the black book began to fall out of use when courts viewed them as a sign that directors were ruling out possibly beneficial takeovers before they even materialized. The result has been disappearance of a physical list but maintenance of a mental one that can't be evidence in court.

As defense strategies have increased, so has the slang to describe "anti-takeover measures." The slang words present a variety of images: *threshold deterrents, sand-bagging, porcupine defenses, bulletproofing,* and the phrase most in vogue in the mid-1980s, *shark repellent.*

The measures, fashioned by hired guns, usually require amending a corporation's charter. In one defense, a corporation arranges for a staggered board, a board of directors in which a certain number are elected each year to prevent outsiders from taking over more than a minority of the board in one year. Another popular shark repellent requires that a "supermajority" such as seventy-five or ninety percent of the shareholders approve any merger. A fair-price amendment prevents the raider from offering different prices to different stockholders.

In a more aggressive approach, a corporation starts acquiring other companies to make itself harder to swallow. A technique called *safe harbor* involves acquiring subsidiaries in heavily regulated industries such as broadcasting. Such industries would require endless amounts of paperwork for a would-be raider. (Safe harbor or *safe haven* also refers to being bought by a congenial white knight who provides safety in the storm of takeover.)

Instead of buying, the corporation may accumulate a *war chest* of money toward future purchases that would make it look less attractive. When CBS was threatened by Ted Turner in 1985, it announced a $1.5 billion line of credit, interpreted by Wall Street as a war chest. Meanwhile, raiders may be filling their own war chests. The mere sight of a full war chest sometimes convinces a target company not to resist a raid.

Once a raider has sprung the attack, the target must act quickly. With the help of hired guns, it may start looking for a white knight and at the same time launch a *literary counterattack* to enlist the support of shareholders and the public. Such a counterattack has several facets: letters to the shareholders giving reasons for opposing the offer, press releases, newspaper advertisements, and speeches by executives.

Meanwhile, the lawyers for the defense look for *showstoppers,* legal barriers such as antitrust problems that would prevent the merger. A famous attempt to stop the show by raising antitrust questions occurred when Mobil, then the second-largest oil company, made a bid for Conoco, the ninth-largest. Conoco responded with the publicity slogan "Nine and two won't go," calling on the Justice Department to object to the merger on antitrust grounds. The issue remained untested because Du Pont, the white knight in the story, acquired Conoco. Raiders have fought several such heated battles over oil companies, in the so-called *oil patch,* for reasons explained by the Wall Street saying, "The cheapest way to strike oil is to buy an oil company."

SCORCHING THE EARTH

In many raids, the target resorts to drastic measures called *scorched-earth defenses.* The name comes from the military tactic of destroying everything that might be useful to an advancing enemy, as proclaimed by Joseph Stalin against the Nazis in 1941:

> We must organize a merciless fight. The enemy must not lay hands on a single means of transport, on a single loaf of bread, on a single liter of fuel. Collective farmers must drive their livestock away and remove their grain. What cannot be removed must be destroyed. Bridges must be dynamited. Forests and depots must be burned down. Intolerable conditions must be created for the enemy.

Wall Street has developed two approaches to conducting a scorched-earth defense. In one, the target makes conditions intolerable for the enemy before he advances very far. In the other, the target takes steps to make itself so unattractive that the raider's goal will not be worth attaining.

When American Express made a bid for McGraw-Hill in 1979, Harold McGraw, Jr., chairman of the target company, used the first approach by responding with verbal gunfire. He attacked the offer as "illegal" and "reckless," and then directed his fire at American Express itself, raising embarrassing questions about the integrity of certain of its past actions. Turning the heat up, McGraw accused the president of American Express of using his position on McGraw-Hill's board to plan his "conspiratorial" raid on the publishing company. The dramatic defense turned the enemy back; American Express let its offer expire, and McGraw-Hill retained its independence.

Other targets have also triumphed by digging up skeletons in the raider's closet and making the takeover too hot to handle. Mead Corporation fought off Occidental Petroleum with publicity about such corporate secrets as illegal campaign contributions, improper overseas payments, and the attempted cover-up of the toxic-waste controversy at Love Canal. In the end, Occidental retreated with its reputation in shreds.

More often, the target makes changes at home to deter the unfriendly suitor. Some of the scorched-earth techniques are arranged to go into effect only in the event that the raider succeeds in the takeover, whereas others begin the self-destruction before the enemy takes control.

A classic scorched-earth defense, the *crown jewel option,* consists of a company selling its most desirable subsidiary, "the jewel in its crown." If the raider has indicated that this prized asset is motivating the takeover, the sale of it kills his interest in the company, but the company pays the price of sacrificing its crown jewel. When Whittaker Corporation was pursuing Brunswick, the target sold its Sherwood Medical Industries, the key division that Whittaker was seeking, and Whittaker withdrew its offer. Sometimes the target promises a potential white knight a *lock-up,* an option to buy a crown jewel; meant to ward off raids, such an arrangement does not always hold up in court.

Two of the most original defenses have been devised by Joseph Flom, a takeover specialist at the law firm of Skadden, Arps, Slate, Meagher & Flom, whose expertise has gained him the title *King of the Takeovers.* In 1975 he crafted the now legendary *Jewish dentist defense* for Sterndent, a dental supply house. Sterndent was defending itself against Magus Corporation, and Flom exploited the fact that Kuwaiti investors partly owned Magus. Flom called to arms the dentists and precious-metal dealers who did business with Sterndent, many of whom were Jewish and would not want to continue business with an Arab-held company. The defense conveyed to Magus that if it took over Sterndent, it would get a crippled company, not a prize. Meanwhile, Flom recruited a white knight. Whether it was the competing offer or the likelihood of Sterndent losing the business of Jewish customers, Magus changed its mind.

In a similar tactic, Flom made the prospect of acquiring a publishing company unattractive by rallying the company's authors to its defense. A character in the 1984 novel *The Takers* describes this *vanishing author* ploy:

> It's a famous stunt Joe Flom pulled some years ago. . . . He was representing Houghton Mifflin when Western Pacific Industries had designs on the company. Flom got a bunch of Houghton Mifflin's best-known authors to say they'd take their talents elsewhere if the company was acquired. Eventually, Western Pacific backed off.[3]

As Western Pacific chairman Howard Newman explained it, he proclaimed the cease-fire because he began to think, "I'm going to buy this company and I ain't going to have nothing."

One scorched-earth technique designed to make the target difficult to swallow and therefore unappetizing has been dubbed the *poison pill.* Wall Streeters attribute the first use of the phrase to either takeover lawyer Martin Lipton or investment banker Martin Siegel, although both deny coining it. Martin Lipton invented the first form of the pill in 1983 when Lennox Inc. was fending off Brown-Forman Distillers. Lennox responded to the hostile bid by issuing convertible preferred stock to its shareholders. Had Brown-Forman succeeded in taking over Lennox against its will, the shareholders could have converted the preferred stock into stock in the remaining entity, Brown-Forman, thus diluting the new company's control. However, Lennox ended up dissolving the pill and accepting a bid from Brown-Forman.

Another famous poison pill, issued by Household International, gave the shareholders of common stock the right to buy one percent of a share of new junior preferred stock for $100. Two *triggering* devices could *spring* the rights: purchase by a single investor of 20 percent or more of the company's stock, or a tender offer for at least 30 percent of the stock. Since either such event spelled doom to the company, the pill was nicknamed the *doomsday pill.* Household shareholders also received *flipover* rights to buy the hostile purchaser's shares at half price in the case of a merger or the transfer of 50 percent of Household's assets to the raider. This would dilute the new company's control and inflate the cost of the acquisition to the raider.

The poison pill takes it name from the cyanide capsule that spies purportedly carry to swallow if caught by the enemy. In Wall Street parlance, a *cyanide capsule* is a large loan that must be repaid immediately if the company is acquired. Similarly, Revlon Corporation issued what some called a *suicide pill,* which, if activated by a takeover, would give the shareholders the right to exchange their shares for debt securities issued by Revlon, thus limiting the acquirer's ability to survive.

Modeled on the poison pill but billed as sweet to everyone except a raider, a *lollipop* or *sugar pill* measure allows shareholders to sell their stocks back to the company at a premium. Great Lake International devised a lollipop when Itel Corporation was buying up its stock, which specified that all shareholders except Itel could take advantage of the offer to sell shares back.

MORE DEFENSES:
FROM GREENMAIL TO FREEZEOUT

By early 1984, the word **greenmail** dominated conversations about takeover defense. Previously known as **paying ransom** or, more romantically, the **goodbye kiss,** greenmail means the repurchase of stock by a target company from an unwanted suitor at higher than market price—buying the raider off, in other words. In 1985, William Safire addressed the word's origin in his weekly column on language:

> "Greenmail is patterned on blackmail, with the green representing greenbacks," reports Sol Steinmetz, a lexicographer, of Barnhart Books. "It may have been inspired by the earlier gray-mail." That is a threat by a defense attorney to force the government to drop an espionage case by demanding the exposure of secrets.[4]

(Another piece of financial slang with the same pattern is **white-mail,** which describes elaborately concealed large corporate bribes.)

Although some **greenmailers** claim they sincerely want to buy the companies in question, Wall Street buzzes with rumors about ones who purposely seek the payoff, **greenmailing** management by threatening to continue a raid unless quickly bought out at a premium. Typically, stockholders decry greenmail because it gives the raider a price the stockholder cannot get, while usually depressing the market price. Critics of greenmail accuse managements of saving their own skins at the expense of the corporation and its shareholders.

To ward off such criticism, threatened managements have concocted **camomail,** camouflaged greenmail, sometimes dubbed **hushmail.** When Chesebrough-Pond's not only redeemed 5 percent of their stock from major greenmailer Carl Icahn (known as **Icahn the Terrible**) but also bought one of his companies at twice its estimated value, observers called the purchase camomail. In a more insidious form of camomail, the public never learns who the greenmailer is. If the raider acquires just under five percent of the target's stock and doesn't have to file with the SEC, the target and the greenmailer may negotiate in secret with an agreement not to reveal names.

Another weapon in the arsenal of scorched-earth defenses received its name from a popular video game: the **Pac-Man strategy,** summed up by the advice, "Eat your opponent before he eats you." As a takeover defense, it means making a counter tender offer for the raiding company's stock. The nickname was bestowed in August 1982 when Martin Marietta counterbid for the stock of Bendix Corporation, the company raiding it. Because such a defense could only be executed by accumulating debt, it falls into the category of scorched earth. More often than not, targets employ the Pac-Man move, also known as the **biteback,** as a delay tactic rather than a serious bid.

Four corporations eventually entered into the Bendix-Martin Marietta battle, nicknamed **The Bill and Mary Show** for the roles played by Bendix CEO William Agee and his controversial assistant at the time, Mary Cunningham, later his wife. The fray, which the press followed closely, brought the slang term **golden parachute** to the forefront of financial news. Designed to cushion the blow of a takeover, a golden parachute is an agreement to pay an executive salary and benefits for a designated number of years if the company falls into the hands of a raider. Although it is not their main function, golden parachutes may serve as a scorched-earth defense in that the raiding company will acquire the debt of the executives' salaries.

Once Martin Marietta had been attacked, its board voted to give golden parachutes to the top twenty-nine executives, and when Martin Marietta initiated its Pac-Man defense, the board of Bendix agreed to parachutes for its executives. In the end, Bendix merged with its rescuer Allied Corporation, and Agee quickly pulled the rip cord on his golden parachute—to collect 4.1 million dollars over five years.

In 1985, Wall Street carried the parachute image one step beyond gold when the proposed payment for Michael Dingman of

Signal was so large that insiders called it a **platinum parachute.** The phrase **golden parachute** comes from **golden handcuffs,** coined in 1976 to mean employment contracts written to keep executives on the job and preserve the continuity of the organization. An earlier term is **golden handshake,** a British expression since 1960 for a lucrative severance package.

Golden parachutes protect the organization in that, when a merger would be in the company's best interest, executives with financial security are less likely to resist the proposal. The parachutes eliminate the executives' fear of **body rain,** leaving them free to concentrate on the business at hand. Body rain, a bit of black humor from Wall Street, refers to the executives who end up desperately walking the streets looking for new jobs as the result of a takeover, merger, or failure in their business.

The phrase comes from the suicides that occur on Wall Street during financial depressions, when businessmen throw themselves from office windows. Although few such deaths have actually been reported, all Wall Streeters have heard about them in legends or even jokes. As a result of the 1929 crash, a joke made the rounds about the hotel clerk who asked guests, "You want a room for sleeping or for jumping?" The depressed market of 1962 prompted the sardonic advice to those walking in the financial district to stay close to the buildings—to avoid falling bodies.

In one takeover defense that avoids body rain and other bloodshed, a publicly held corporation **goes private,** a move known as a **freezeout.** One shareholder or a group of shareholders pays cash, debt, or preferred stock to buy the company's common stock from members of the public who own it. Having taken the company out of play, the management no longer has to worry about raiders, who are effectively left out in the cold. Not all embattled companies can or want to execute a freezeout, but for those who do, it is the ultimate takeover defense. Although a private company may still enter the fray as a black or white knight, it can avoid being a victim of this latest financial craze—with its melodrama, romance, and machoism—known on Wall Street as **takeover fever** or **merger mania.**

7

Swindles and Scandals

Dear Abby, I've met the most wonderful boy, and I'm terribly in love with him. We're engaged and plan to be married, but I have this terrible problem. He doesn't know about my family; my father's in jail, my mother's running a house of prostitution, my sister is a prostitute there, and my brother is a stockbroker. Dare I tell him about my brother?

This joke, while it exaggerates the shady image of stockbrokers, hits home because since its beginning, the stock market and its inhabitants have been caught up in a host of swindles, scandals, and other illegal activities. In the mid-1980s, with its stunning *insider trading* scandals, the joke-teller could plug in "my brother is an arb," or "my brother is an investment banker" to draw a laugh.

THE KING OF THE ARBS FALLS

Ivan Boesky, Martin Siegel, and Dennis Levine—an arb and two investment bankers—played the star roles in the scandal that stretched through 1986 and 1987, staggering Wall Street with its immensity. Levine and Siegel exploited their positions in mergers and acquisitions departments, in which they advised companies concerning takeovers, and each leaked the confidential, non-public knowledge to Boesky, Wall Street's *King of the Arbs,* who traded on it and made millions.

The web of intrigue untangled by the SEC started with Dennis Levine and a ring of his cohorts. At the time of his arrest, Levine worked as a senior merger specialist at Drexel Burnham, where he evidently found his earnings of more than a million dollars inadequate. At Drexel and previous firms where he worked, Levine beefed up his salary and bonuses through illegal trading, gleaning $12.6 million dollars in five years on an original investment of $170,000. Unknown to him, Levine's secret artifice began to totter when Merrill Lynch received an anonymous letter from Caracas, Venezuela, which claimed brokers in the company's Caracas office were trading on inside information. Those brokers pointed to a broker in the New York office, who insisted that he had modeled his trades in question on one of his accounts, Bank Leu International in the Bahamas, where the SEC uncovered Levine's name.

Once Levine agreed to cooperate with the SEC, the plot thickened as he fingered eleven other Wall Streeters. According to rumor, in order to trap his former colleagues, Levine made telephone calls on phony pay telephones, which had the prerecorded jingle of coins and the sound of operator instructions, while the U.S. Attorney's office was listening in. Boesky, best-known and wealthiest of the Street's arbitrageurs, was the biggest fish Levine helped the SEC to pull in.

It turned out that Levine had initially given Boesky free tips and when those paid off, the two of them set up a formal arrangement in which Levine was to receive a certain percentage of the profit. However, Boesky put off paying Levine the $2.4 million due him from the successes, until Levine's arrest made it too late; noting the lack of honor among thieves, some doubt Boesky would ever have paid up or given Levine the presidency of Boesky's investment firm, as he had apparently promised.

The jokes on Wall Street after Levine's May 12th, 1986, arrest and the news that he was cooperating with the authorities, revealed the uneasiness and resentment the arbs felt.

Did you hear the new definition of an arb? Someone who has never met, or spoken to, Dennis Levine.

———————

First Arb: You going to the concert tonight?
Second Arb: No, who's singing?
First Arb: Dennis Levine

(The wordplay here hinges on *singing* as general slang for acting as a stool pigeon.)

The legendary Boesky, in turn, implicated Martin Siegel, a thirty-eight-year-old Wall Street whiz kid known for his prowess in defending corporations against takeovers. As the story of Boesky and Siegel unfolded, with its codewords and couriers, the resemblance to a spy novel was striking. The two men would get in touch by telephone, using the signal "Let's have coffee" to mean one had information to share. Siegel would meet a courier from Boesky in a public place, greet him with a secret password, and receive from him the payment for tips—a briefcase full of cash. As if to maintain the level of drama, on November 14, 1986, federal marshals burst in on Siegel at lawyer Martin Lipton's office, where the two were meeting, and thrust a subpoena at him, a subpoena that the investment banker could see spelled the end of his career. Although Siegel had at one time been known as the **Monk of Wall Street** because he didn't smoke or drink, his part in the scandal, which caught many observers by surprise, shattered his reputation.

FOUNDED IN FRAUD

Shattered reputations, like Siegel's, are nothing new in the stock market. In 1719 Daniel Defoe, author of *Robinson Crusoe*, expressed the same sentiment as the Dear Abby parody, but in much stronger terms, and critics of Wall Street today might contend that his words castigating British stockbrokers could be redirected at inside traders. Defoe described the brokers' work as such:

A complete system of knavery; . . . it is a trade founded in
fraud, born of deceit, and nourished by trick, treat, wheedle,
forgeries, falsehoods, and all sorts of delusions; coining false
news . . . whispering imaginary terrors, frights, hopes, [and]
expectations.

Many a disgruntled customer since 1719 has heard the whis-
pered hopes, then fallen victim to "all sorts of delusions" in the
stock market; and more than one United States President has attacked Wall Streeters as knaves who ill-served the country. During the Civil War, speculators planted spies in the Confederate
army to ferret out battle plans as an indicator of how gold prices
would move, infuriating President Lincoln. "What do you think
of those fellows in Wall Street who are gambling gold at such a
time as this?" Lincoln is said to have asked, adding, "For my part,
I wish every one of them had his devilish head shot off."

Eighty-some years later, when the need for food in Europe
after World War II drove up grain prices on the commodity exchanges, an angry President Truman called the commodities
traders, "merchants of human misery" and, in an effort to shame
them, published a list of those who held positions of more than
two million bushels of grain.

Even among professional criminals, the stock market has been
held in ill repute. Legend has it that mobster Al Capone once
remarked, "It's a racket. Those stock market guys are crooked."
And a dictionary of underworld slang published in 1935 records
that one way to describe "a respectable girl" was to say of her,
"She isn't listed on the stock market."

RIGGING THE MARKET

The late nineteenth and early twentieth centuries offered golden
opportunities for making money in ways that later became illegal.
Wily, unscrupulous market players, alone or in groups, **rigged
the market** again and again by manipulating prices to make a
profit. As a 1911 writer explains,

When the stock market has been "rigged" it is understood that
events have been made to transpire in accordance with the wishes
of those powerful enough to effect such results. A trap is rigged
to catch the unwary animal; the market is rigged to catch the
unwary speculator or investor.[1]

The slang word *rig* does not appear to be derived from the
nautical term; rather, it is related to *thimblerig,* the name of a
swindling game played like the shell game or three-card monte
seen on the streets of New York City today. *The Rogues and Rogueries of New York,* published in 1865, describes the thimblerig,
which it reports was played at the racetrack, "at the ball or cricket
grounds at Hoboken," and "now and then near the Central Park."

> The apparatus is . . . a small stand, three brass thimbles and
> a little ball resembling, in size and appearance, a green pea.
> . . . The "Rigger," in the most *nonchalant* manner imagin-
> able, places the ball apparently under one of the thimbles in
> plain view of the spectators, and offers to bet any sum that "it
> isn't there."[2]

Typically, a bystander—who is actually the rigger's accomplice—
steps forward, places a bet, and wins, convincing a greenhorn in
the crowd to risk his money on the apparently easy game, and
inevitably, lose.

Around the turn of the century, Wall Streeters borrowed the
name for this swindle and applied it to the stock market, using
thimblerigging the market interchangeably with **rigging the market,** and **thimblerigger** to describe the market manipulator.

Although some members of the public cried out against the
unfairness of big operators rigging the market, which many compared to playing with loaded dice, others defended the practice.
These small investors, like those who bet on three-card monte,
hoped to outsmart the manipulators (or imitate their trades) and
turn a profit thanks to the thimblerig.

To set market traps, the manipulators banded together in **pools,** *cliques,* and *rings.* The first pool appeared on the scene in 1791, organized to manipulate stock of the U.S. Bank. Members of a pool contributed money, which was handed over to a single operator, who put into effect various strategies and subterfuges. He could depress the price of a stock, buy a lot at the low point, then artificially raise the price, and sell at a profit; or he might sell short, then depress the price and make a profit. Often the operator enlisted the help of financial columnists to spread rumors about the stock's worth, "coining false news" in Defoe's words. Another ploy required influence with the directors of the company in question, who would declare a stock dividend at a key moment to ignite interest in the stock. Pool members shared the profits, or if the operator's rigging failed, the losses.

Best known of the pool operators was **Silent Henry** Keep, known for his reticence and described by contemporaries as a "man of honor, of unblenching integrity," although by today's standards his work would call forth indictments from the SEC. While managing other people's money, Keep advanced his own fortunes in a rags-to-riches story, starting life as the son of a town pauper and leaving an estate of four million dollars when he died.

In one common arrangement, the **blind pool,** members remained ignorant of how the operator spent the funds. Beyond initial instructions, they had no say in management, because secrecy made it easier to succeed in rigging the market. The **bobtail pool,** another variation, was an informal group of investors who loosely agreed to manipulate a certain stock, without using a manager; members could withdraw from the pool at will. Similarly, **combinations, rings,** and **cliques** acted in concert to manipulate the market, but without formal agreements and without central managers. All such groups, formal or informal, are now banned by the SEC.

The manipulators made money by **milking the Street,** depressing a price through selling and rumor, buying at a low point, then raising it again and selling at the top. In 1871, Matthew Smith described Wall Street's reaction to the ploy:

The street is in a maze. Speculators are puzzled. Dealers are bothered. Men cannot tell what to do. Stocks are rushed up and down rapidly. In the excitement the combination reap a golden harvest. They have milked the street.[3]

Today, the slang term **to milk** means to obtain as much money or profits as possible from a person or company, "milking them dry."

Operators also resorted to **gunning a stock,** already an old expression by 1900, and **ballooning a stock,** also from the nineteenth century. Gunning means to create an artificial downward trend, and ballooning, an upward trend. **Hot-air specialties** were what Wall Streeters called ballooned stocks in the 1920s, full of hot air from overblown promotions. Such ballooning inspired Will Rogers' wry comment, "There's a proverb on Wall Street: What goes up—must have been sent up by somebody."

SWINGING A CORNER

As a cat corners a mouse and toys with it before the kill, so the bulls and bears try to corner their competitors in perhaps the best known of market manipulations, **the corner,** an expression that dates back to 1849. Most prevalent in the second half of the nineteenth century and the early 1900s, but not yet obsolete, **cornering the market** consists of buying up the floating supply of a stock that other speculators have sold short. When the short sellers need to acquire the stock to fulfill their contracts, they cannot get any. Those who have **swung the corner** can demand exorbitant prices from the short sellers, thus **squeezing the shorts,** as it's called. Wall Streeters used to speak of bears being **caught in a corner** or **driven into a corner,** like the mouse.

Corners did not begin on the stock market. In ancient Greece, a philosopher named Thales, observing one year that the olive harvest promised to be especially bountiful, cornered the market in olive presses, necessary to make oil, then sold them to the growers at harvest time for a goodly profit. History also shows that

German families in the sixteenth century tried, without success, to corner the markets in quicksilver and pepper.

In their heyday, corners became more than just financial ventures; they turned into obsessions and personal vendettas, as market writer Edwin Lefevre explained in 1923:

> A wise old broker told me that all the big operators of the '60s and '70s had one ambition, and that was to work a corner. In many cases this was the offspring of vanity; in others, the desire for revenge. At all events, to be pointed out as the man who had successfully cornered this or the other stock was in reality recognition of brains, boldness and boodle.[4]

Frank Norris's 1902 novel *The Pit* illustrates this ambition, describing a massive corner on wheat at the Chicago Board of Trade. The main character Curtis Jadwin has the larger-than-life quality of the era's robber barons, and his corner in wheat takes on mythic proportions. When Jadwin and his broker realize what they can do on the market, it was

> as though a veil had been ripped asunder, as though an explosion had rushed through the air upon them, deafening, blinding. Jadwin sprang forward, gripping the broker by his shoulder.
>
> "Sam," he shouted, "do you know—great God!—do you know what this means? Sam, we can corner the market."[5]

Jadwin *jackscrewed* or *jacked up* the market, forcing prices up to unnatural levels and keeping them there artificially. But due to an unexpectedly huge harvest of wheat, the corner *broke* under him and when it did, the short sellers rejoiced in their triumph and his destruction:

> The great corner smashed! Jadwin busted! They themselves saved, saved, saved! Cheer followed upon cheer, yell after yell. Hats went up into the air. In a frenzy of delight men danced and leaped and capered upon the edge of the Pit.[6]

Norris was not exaggerating the intensity of emotions that could be created by a corner, in which manipulators mercilessly **turned the screws** on the shorts to make as much profit as they possibly could, regardless of the consequences to others. When Jim Fisk and Jay Gould tried to corner the market in gold in 1869 and nearly succeeded, one short seller committed suicide before the government intervened in the market and the corner crumbled.

Although, in this case, the government officials protected investors, at other times, the government's intervention and that of the courts was aimed at personal profit and not at maintaining a fair market. Operators attempting a corner would solicit the aid of city councils and judges; Jim Fisk, according to one writer, owned "several railroads and steamboats, an opera house, [and] at least one bench of judges."

During the first Harlem corner, New York City councilmen foolishly believed that they could out-manipulate Commodore Vanderbilt in the market. Vanderbilt had come to the council for permission to build a certain railroad line that would raise the price of Harlem stock. The council granted his request, then sold Harlem stock short, planning to repeal the ordinance, and so profit when the stock fell. But Vanderbilt caught wind of the scheme and bought up all the Harlem stock, so that when the ordinance was repealed, the stock price fell a little temporarily and then he pushed it up and up, cornering the councilmen and their friends to the tune of several million dollars. In a show of stupidity, the state Legislature tried the same trick with the Commodore and lost even more money. Losses on the two corners were so steep that for years afterward, market players used the expression **He went short of Harlem** to describe abject poverty.

WASHING AND LAUNDERING

Wall Streeters not powerful enough to rig the market can manipulate stock on a smaller scale through **wash sales,** a term from 1848. In **washing** a stock, two or more speculators buy and sell the same stock simultaneously in order to stir up interest in it.

The seller and buyer, working together, do not exchange money, but the trades are recorded at increasing prices, sure to start rumors about the stock. A stock could be **washed down,** to attract shorts, as well as **washed up.** Exchanges have forbidden wash sales for many years. As early as 1875, one writer explained:

> A Wash Sale is a sham transaction between two brokers for the purpose of influencing the market and making a stock appear active. It is a bluff game, but if detected, the board will inflict a severe penalty.[7]

In a variation on the cleaning theme, slang has also called these sham trades the **laundry business.** At one time, when big operators had artificially pushed the market up, it was said they had **laundried it up;** a character in a 1923 story in *The Saturday Evening Post* remarked, "At times the washing was too crude to deceive anyone. The brokers had no hesitation in saying that 'the laundry was active' whenever anybody tried to wash up some stock or other."[8] In later examples, one slang dictionary lists as 1930s slang **to be a launderer,** meaning "to commit a stock exchange washing," and a 1935 underworld dictionary defines **laundry** as "mining or stock exchange (where one gets a good cleaning)."[9]

Laundering money, and its synonym **money-washing,** now mean the practice of channeling illegally obtained funds through several financial institutions to make them appear legitimate. The terms gained popularity during the Watergate scandal of 1972–74, in which money was laundered through Mexican banks.

When the ticker tape came into use, a new name arose for an action similar to the **wash sale**: **painting the tape.** Since each stock transaction with its amount and price appears on the ticker tape, when speculators conspire to produce fictitious sales, these too appear; thus the conspirators "paint the tape" to catch the eye, and pocketbook, of tape-worms.

Despite rules as early as 1820 against fictitious sales, exchanges still detect them occasionally. In 1984, *The Wall Street Journal* reported that the Kansas City Board of Trade fined ten traders, saying it had " 'reason to believe' that the traders may have been involved in illegal 'wash-sale' trading between 1982 and early 1983."

Today wash sale also refers to selling stock at a loss within thirty days of buying it, then buying it again with the intent of claiming a capital loss for tax purposes—a claim not allowed by the Internal Revenue Service.

BUCKET SHOPS AND BOILER ROOMS

A shady Wall Streeter could combine legitimate business with an occasional foray into wash sales or painting the tape, without devoting all his time to fraud. But those with no patience for earning money honestly have created bucket shops and boiler rooms, establishments for fraudulent sales of stocks and commodities. The first *bucket shops* connected with trading opened in Chicago in the 1870s. At first these shops dealt in small amounts of grains, to cater to small customers once the Chicago Board of Trade required a minimum order of 5,000 bushels of grain. The term then expanded to apply to offices that resembled brokerages but were actually just gambling establishments. Around the same time, the phrase bucket shops also described dives where customers could buy their evening supply of cheap beer, in buckets or pitchers.

Folk etymology suggests that the buckets for the grain gave the shops their name, although as often as not, no grain exchanged hands in the betting process. Another theory has it that the name was borrowed from the shops that sold beer in buckets. However, the *Oxford English Dictionary* gives an 1812 definition for *to bucket* as "to cheat, swindle," which could well explain the origin of "bucket shop," where swindling held sway. Under its definition for "bucket shop," the *Oxford English Dictionary* quotes an 1886 publication that ties the shops to thimblerigging:

> There are 'bucket shops' and 'bucket shops.' The worst class of
> them are thimble and pea sharpers under a more polite name.

In the bucket shops that resemble stock brokerages, a *bucketeer* took orders from customers but did not execute them, instead betting against the customer. The transaction amounted to gambling. The odds greatly favored the bucketeer, who added to his easy money by charging commissions as a legitimate broker does. Taking the swindle one step further, bucketeers often manipulated prices to ensure that customers lost. If the bucket shop itself suffered too many losses, it would simply close up one night and open in another place, a fly-by-night aspect that still characterizes fraudulent sales of commodities. As a spokesman for the Commodity Futures Trading Commission, which regulates commodity sales, told a reporter for *The New York Times* in 1985, "The trouble with these bucket shops is that when you shut one down, the owners scatter and start up new firms in other states. It's like hitting mercury with a hammer."

A related setting for snaring unwary investors is the *boiler room,* a term now used interchangeably with bucket shop, although in the past a *boiler room* was sometimes just one of the rooms in a larger bucket shop. Lore has it that a New Englander named Archie Andrews opened the first boiler room around 1910 when he shrewdly recognized the potential of the telephone-in sales. In a *boiler room,* aggressive salesmen—and, today, women—telephone potential customers and try to snag them with a high-pressure sales pitch, sometimes referred to as the *razz.* Some contend that this "high-pressure" aspect of the business inspired the name *boiler room,* while others say it came into use because the noise of so many voices on the telephones gives the room the sound of a boiler room. A more mundane etymology suggests the low-budget enterprises did in fact start in basement rooms with boilers in them.

Typically, boiler-room operators work from sucker lists to sell speculative stocks, options, or commodities. Despite efforts to close them down, boiler rooms have survived and even thrived, especially during the 1920s, when any stock would sell, and the 1950s, when penny stocks dominated the business. Similarly, during the 1970s, telephone swindles to sell London commodity options reached such a volume in the U.S. that the Commodity Futures

Trading Commission banned sales of the options, only to have the boiler rooms switch to fraudulent sales in diamonds, Scotch whiskey, and silver.

Boiler rooms show no signs of becoming extinct. An article in *Consumer Reports* magazine, May 1987, warned against rampant "telefraud," fraudulent investment sales over the telephone that push precious metals, oil and gas leases, currency contracts, art prints, rare coins, and anything else that gullible customers will buy—only to find out later that they have been duped out of their money.

COXEYS, YAKS, AND DYNAMITERS

A lexicon of colorful words has been created over the years to describe the inhabitant of boiler rooms—from **yaks** to **needlemen.** All those who make the phony investment calls are dubbed yaks or **yackers;** since they spend their days talking, their slang name no doubt comes from the general slang terms *to yak*, meaning to talk idly, and *yackety-yak*, "stupid chatter."

Yaks can be divided into categories of skill. For example, a **coxey** (sometimes spelled **cocksy**) or **fronter,** an inexperienced seller, makes the first or **front** call to a prospective customer, working from a telephone list, to determine if the person called may want to open an account. The coxey tries to convince the person to make a small investment. In the lingo of the yak, when a boiler-room operator phones a prospect, he is **stoking the boiler.**

Before calls are made or after the first call, the boiler-room operators like to send out promotional literature, called **hot stuff** or simply **paper.** Victims inadvertently fall into the boiler-room trap by responding to newspaper advertisements that offer free brochures from what appear to be legitimate investment firms. Anyone who succumbs to a sales pitch—due to the hot stuff or a phone call—becomes, in the yaks' slang, a **mooch.**

After the front call comes a phone call from a more experienced con artist. If the potential customer needs convincing, this second yak will suggest calling a **singer,** an alleged satisfied customer who will "sing the praises" of the investment. (*To sing* in general slang means to make a sales pitch, taken from the slang of sidewalk vendors known as pitchmen.) If the mooch has already bought into the scheme, the second caller may be a *reloader,* who has perfected the skill of selling more of the same stock or commodity, in a follow-up telephone conversation dubbed a *load call.* The yak is always happy *to pluck the chicken* again.

Since the 1920s, *dynamiters,* high-pressure salesmen "of extraordinary virulence" (as described by H. L. Mencken), have held the highest positions in the boiler room hierarchy. The term is not limited to investment fraud—dynamiters known as *suede-shoe boys* because of their flashy clothing turned their sales prowess to selling aluminum siding and other "home improvements" during the 1950s.

These fast-talking salesmen would "clip the mooch, and sell the sucker." In underworld slang, a *mooch man* canvasses for the sale of worthless stocks, while a rich businessman too proud to admit he has been duped into buying the shares is a *mooch manna.* (Automobile dealers use *mooch* to describe customers who show up with their calculators in hand, acting under the mistaken belief that they can outsmart the salesmen.)

Working with the dynamiters, *needlemen* specialized in "injecting" in customers the idea of getting rich quickly. And any of the disreputable con artists might have employed a *bird dog, plier* or *tout,* agents who scouted on commission for likely customers, digging up or *bird dogging* information on them for the yak.

THE BIG CON

Dynamiters and reloaders have long relied on honing their verbal skills to cheat investors, but in the heyday of the *big con game,* criminals who specialized in investment fraud needed an entire range of acting skills. Professional swindlers called confidence men (although occasionally women played the big con) organized fake brokerage offices and fictitious stock movements to "con" their victims out of huge amounts of money in a hoax known as *the rag.*

Linguist David Maurer, who was in close touch with the underworld, described the rag in detail in his book *The Big Con.* According to him, the big con games—the rag, the wire, and the payoff—reached their heights between 1914 and 1925. The rag and the payoff were still going strong in 1939, when he wrote his book, but the wire had fallen out of use.

In pulling off the rag, confidence men typically avoided violence, relying instead on their wits, their knowledge of human behavior, and their acting ability. The con game hinged on drawing the *mark,* as the victim was called, into a scheme that he understood was illegal but found too profitable to resist. Involving the mark in illegal action discouraged him from going to the police once he was swindled. As further security against time in prison, con men routinely bribed police and judges in an arrangement known as *the fix.*

Before the rag was invented, con men engaged in another effective, but less lucrative, stock swindle. In it, one con man would pose as a broker and after finding a mark, perhaps on a sucker list, tell him of a stock that was certain to go up soon, according to inside information. The so-called broker would claim that he knew of a poor, dying old man with several thousand shares of that stock who did not realize what it was worth. Having lured in the greedy mark, the con man would propose buying the stock at a low price, selling it, and splitting the profit fifty-fifty, but, he said, he needed the mark to put up the money. Like all confidence games, this one succeeded only if the con man gained the mark's confidence.

Once the confidence was secured, the two would visit a hotel where the second con man acted the part of the dying stockowner. The mark would pay over several thousand dollars and receive the fake securities. He would then be sent off to a large city nearby to sell them, duped by his own greed and stupidity, while the two con men split their profit and disappeared.

The rag, a far more elaborate undertaking, required a fake brokerage office—*the big store*—complete with tickers, telephones, a chalk board for prices, and small-time crooks posing as brokers, clerks, and free-spending customers. First, the *roper* hooked a victim by *telling the tale,* revealing that he knew a man who could give them guaranteed tips about the market. When this man, played by the *insideman,* was introduced, he persuaded the mark that they could make money together. He sealed his argument by lending the mark money to place small orders at the fake brokerage, using the alleged sure tip. Of course, the mark made tidy profits on these trades.

Taken in by the swindlers' generosity and the certainty of the investment, the victim sent home for a large amount of money, after which the three of them went again to the brokerage. There the roper made a transaction with the mark's money and, as part of the scheme, made a major mistake. He bought instead of selling short, and the victim would watch the stock price plunge on the ticker, knowing he had lost all the money. If the victim was gullible enough, the con men would convince him to send for more money, telling him they couldn't possibly miss the second time—but, of course, they did.

To keep the mark from causing trouble, the con men sometimes staged a murder, with the insideman shooting the roper in anger over the expensive mistake. As moviegoers saw in *The Sting,* in which Paul Newman and Robert Redford played confidence men who successfully swindled a victim in the con game *the wire,* the man "shot" had bladders of animal blood that burst and made him appear to bleed to death. Not wanting to be involved in murder, most marks would be only too happy to forget the lost money and rush out of town.

Perhaps the best-known victim of the rag was a Texas rancher named Frank Norfleet. In 1919, five con men lured him into believing they had inside information on the cotton market, and fleeced him twice for a total of $45,000. But unlike other victims, Norfleet fought back. He spent the next three years and a great deal of money tracking down the swindlers, and seeing that they were tried and convicted, except for one who committed suicide.

But the victory proved to be short-lived; within four years, not a single one remained behind bars. As Maurer comments, "Such is the tale of the fix."[10]

THE BROKERAGE FIRM OF "TOUT, TICKER, DICKER, AND CHURN"

This facetious tag for a brokerage house highlights some of the dangers that may beset investors if they deal with an unethical broker. Of all shady brokerage practices, **churning** receives the most publicity. A broker who churns a customer's account makes numerous buy and sell transactions with the object, not of making the customer money, but of piling up commissions. Each trade means a commission for the broker, who knows full well that an account with little action brings him little money. The worst abuses occur when the customer gives the broker considerable or complete control over the trades, enabling an unscrupulous broker to **churn, burn, and bury** the customer—that is, squander the money in the account through risky trades and numerous commissions.

Churning, also known as **switching** and **twisting,** is not always a clear-cut issue. In defending themselves, accused brokers point to customers who have seen confirmation slips on every trade or even been consulted about every trade without voicing objections. They say that the client's greed and impatience prompted the frenzied, highly speculative trading pattern; that with each small loss, the client insisted on trying something new that could reap large profits. A disgruntled broker complains in Murray Bloom's *From Rogues to Riches,*

> There have to be two guilty parties in this kind of transaction: the broker and [the customer] herself. Why should the broker alone be held accountable for her stupidity and greed? Every customer who's churned and lost money is unhappy. If she was churned and made money, there'd be no gripe.[11]

Other businesses besides brokerages are accused of forms of churning. When medical practices require unnecessary visits, it's called churning. When law firms add irrelevant research and motions to their billable hours, slang describes it as churning or *running up the meter*. No wonder that the imaginary brokerage firm **Dewey, Scruem & Howe** has a counterpart in the law firm of Dewey, Cheatem & Howe.

Part of the practice of churning a brokerage customer may be to *tout* a stock, that is, to heap praises on it simply to sell the stock regardless of its worth. A broker, who is called a tout, may promote a particular stock after buying it for her own account, to push the price up, after which the broker sells at a profit, an unethical ploy known as **scalping**.

Similarly, scalping occurs when a firm has all its brokers push a certain stock, with the motive of keeping the price steady while the firm sells its own holdings in that stock. In view of the pitfalls that an investor may encounter, the NYSE advice to its members in Rule 405, "Know your customer," has been turned around by some to read, "Know your broker."

TRICKS IN BLOCK TRADING

As block trading by institutions has come to dominate the market, **tape dancing, capping,** and **front running,** abuses in these elephantine trades, have joined the list of illegal market practices.

The slang term tape dancing, with its whimsical metaphor, applies to manipulative procedure, one that influences buyers through the electronic ticker tape. In it, block traders pay institutional investors one-eighth or one-fourth a point over the last price on the tape for a block of stock. Although the trader charges a higher commission than usual, the institutional investor gains financially through the trick. The potential losers are those who see the trade dancing on the tape, take it to mean that an eager investor bought the block on the uptick, and so rush out under that false impression to buy the stock.

Institutional investors devised capping to protect against losses from selling call options, which are agreements to sell stock at a certain price, the strike price. The buyer will want to exercise the option if the stock price rises above the strike price, so if that occurs, an unscrupulous institutional investor schemes to depress the stock price by dumping large amounts of the stock on the market just before expiration date. After the call has expired, the institutional investor buys back the stock, having made money from selling the option without the usual risk of having it exercised.

When investors or traders get the jump on other investors with advance information about major trades of stock, and exploit that knowledge by buying or selling options in that stock, they are guilty of front running, a practice prohibited at the CBOE and the Merc. In one case of front running that occurred at the CBOE in 1984, less than an hour before call options in the S&P index were due to expire, the index was under 155. If it remained under 155 until the expiration time, the options would be worthless. Consequently, when orders for call options came in at that point, local traders sold them for the low price of six dollars each. Then, according to a report in *Business Week*,

> A couple of minutes before the session ended, block trades in a half-dozen stocks that represent 22% of the S&P 100 were executed in New York. That rallied the index to 155.78; instead of pocketing their $6 fees, the locals wound up losing $72 on each option. Infuriated, they identified three prominent New York investment banking firms as big options buyers and told exchange officials they suspected them of "front-running."[12]

It is difficult, however, to prove such maneuvers are manipulation rather than merely shrewd trading.

TRADING ON THE INSIDE

The most publicized Wall Street offense of the 1980s, **insider trading,** can be as hard to pin down as frontrunning. Even when widespread gossip suggests, as it did about Boesky, that a speculator is succeeding due to dishonesty rather than just shrewdness, the SEC may face a monumental task in proving abuse of inside information.

Before the days of the SEC, the phrase *inside information,* which dates from the 1880s, did not carry the weight it does today. Investors with connections could exploit *inside dope,* as it was also called, as a matter of course, cheered on by the maxim, "A friend in the market is better than money in the chest." For those who didn't have a friend in the market, tipsters ran newspaper advertisements likely to result in a ruined pocketbook. An article titled "Humbugs Labelled 'Business Opportunities' " in *Moody's Magazine,* May, 1906, discussed such an ad, which read:

> Have reliable inside information regarding certain stock market movement to take place at once; can make a lot of money for you quickly off a small amount.
> Address A. K., 623 Herald, stating when and where you may be seen.[13]

The magazine writer comments, "The sort of advertisement shown in this reproduction bears the impress of rascality on its face. Any man who really has inside information as to a stock movement surely violates a trust in telling of it, and is looking for graft."

In the bull market of the 1920s, it seemed that everyone was privy to the inside track on stocks, so much so that inside information became, temporarily, a meaningless phrase. Elizabeth Frazer, writing in 1928, poked fun at gossipy speculators, in a fictitious conversation between two women. In answer to the question, "How do you know which one to pick?" one of the women boasts:

> "Oh, well, of course you have to have inside information and that's what I have. You see, my chauffeur and the chauffeur of Mr. B."—she mentioned a name prominent in financial circles—"are bosom buddies, and so I just ask George, my chauffeur, to ask his buddy to ask Mr. B. for the low-down on any

stock I'm interested in, and so I get my information first-hand."[14]

Hence, Bernard Baruch's much-quoted advice, "Beware of barbers, beauticians, waiters—or anyone else—bringing gifts of 'inside information.' "

But with the establishment of the SEC, inside information ceased to mean wild tips from chauffeurs and took on a more technical definition. It now refers to statistics, financial reports, rules changes, upcoming events, and the like, that would influence trading in a security and that has not been publicly announced. This "material, non-public information," as the SEC often terms it, is typically available to company directors and officers, their advisers including investment bankers and lawyers, and stockholders who own enough stock to influence the market in it. For these players, trading on this information, known only to a few, is clearly insider trading, punishable by law.

But Wall Streeters complain that they cannot always know if they are committing insider trading. Critics of the SEC contend that the definition, which they call hazy, allows the commission to spread its net too wide, prosecuting those whose status as an insider is not clear-cut or who trade based on knowledge that does not strictly fit the usual definition of inside information.

For example, in the famous case of 1973 Equity Funding (which, the joke goes, was a company without equity or funds), the SEC charged Raymond Dirks with insider trading, even though he was not employed by Equity Funding. Dirks, a security analyst, uncovered the company's faulty finances, but before he informed the SEC, he advised his clients to sell their holdings in Equity. Although some commended Dirks for his astuteness in detecting the fraud and his courage in blowing the whistle, the SEC contended that he committed insider trading in informing his clients before the news was made available to the public. Ultimately the U.S. Supreme Court disagreed, because Dirks was not a fiduciary of the company, and overturned the decision.

More recently, the SEC won a conviction, also scheduled to

be heard by the Supreme Court, against *Wall Street Journal* reporter R. Foster Winans, whose influential column "Heard on the Street" provided him with a trading tool he couldn't resist. According to Winans, stockbroker Peter Brant first hatched the plot whereby Winans would pass along names of stocks to be mentioned favorably in upcoming columns. Brant would buy the stock, the friendly words would send the price up, and the two conspirators would split the profits.

The plan's execution, however, was fraught with blunders, such as Winans forgetting his code name of "Howard Cohen" when he called to give Brant tips. Brant undermined secrecy by bringing in another broker and a client, and he traded so heavily in the stocks Winans promoted that investigators noticed. Although Winans did not technically possess inside information, the SEC, contending that trading on stolen information is illegal, argued that Winans is guilty because he had "misappropriated" the information from the newspaper.

In the old days, the big danger from counting on inside tips was financial; as the proverb warned, "Inside information and a long pocketbook have ruined many a man." Today, it's the illegality of using them that makes gifts of inside information perilous to Wall Streeters. Winans awaits the Supreme Court's decision, Dennis Levine is in prison, Boesky and Siegel are about to be sentenced, and an array of other famous Wall Street names have been drawn into the investigation. Whether big operators such as Boesky have lost or gained financially through their illegal trading, even after paying fines, remains unclear. Nevertheless, the mighty are fallen and, as a result, Wall Street itself has suffered once again from a tainted image. This association with the criminal that haunts the Street prompted a joke that made the rounds at the height of the scandal:

Q. What happens when you cross a pig with a Wall Streeter?
A. There are some things that even a pig won't do.

8

Exchanges and Brokerages of the Gold-Paved Street

THE NOTORIOUS THOROUGHFARE

Physically, Wall Street is a short street, laid out between the East River and Trinity Church—its inhabitants describe it, somewhat ominously, as "having a river at one end and a graveyard at the other." But in effect the *Gold-Paved Street,* as it's been called, stretches long and wide, encompassing the financial establishment in New York and the securities and commodities business throughout the United States; the words "Wall Street'" have long meant more than the name of a street in Manhattan.

To some, Wall Street represents the possibility of becoming wealthy. Those dreamers have christened the street, with its towering buildings, the *Golden Canyon,* calling up the legends that streets in the New World were paved with gold. But those who have lost money on Wall Street have disparaged it as the *Street of Sorrows,* and H. L. Mencken condemned it as "the devil's chasm."

As one who wanted to see the dream spread throughout the country, Charles Merrill, founder of Merrill Lynch, waxed lyrical about the larger meaning of Wall Street in a newspaper advertisement he ran during the 1948 presidential campaign. Merrill complained that President Truman had trotted out "the moth-eaten bogey of a Wall Street tycoon," and went on,

> Mr. Truman knows as well as anybody that there isn't any Wall Street. That's just legend. Wall Street is Montgomery Street in San Francisco. Seventeenth Street in Denver. Marietta Street in Atlanta. Federal Street in Boston. Main Street in Waco, Texas. And it's any spot in Independence, Missouri, where thrifty people go to invest their money, to buy and sell securities.

But, in contrast to Merrill's positive use of Wall Street as a metaphor, comedian Will Rogers sided with those who dubbed it **Wailing Wall Street:** "I dident [sic] have anything particular against Wall Street, but knowing the geographical and physical attributes of the street, I knew that it was crooked. You can stand at the head of it and you can only see to the bend."

If you did stand at the head of Wall Street, physically instead of metaphorically, you would be standing in front of the imposing Trinity Church, which has played a role in Wall Street folklore since the parish was founded in 1697. Wall Streeters even incorporate it into their jokes—like this one that made the rounds during the insider trading scandals of the 1980s—to signal that they're talking about the financial district:

> Two drunks are lurching through the graveyard at Trinity Church when one of them stumbles into a gravestone. He squints at it and reads the epitaph, "Here lies an investment banker and an honest man." The drunk turns to his friend and, shaking his head, says, "Can you believe it? This place is getting so crowded that now they're burying 'em two to a grave."

The traders' tendency to nickname their fellows has also extended to the church; *Moody's Magazine* noted in 1910 that Wall Streeters had dubbed Reverend William Wilkinson, minister at Trinity Church, the **Bishop of Wall Street.** During the 1920s, a

Wall Street saying claimed that a man seen entering Trinity Church was a man in trouble.

The name Wall Street comes from a wooden wall, or stockade, erected in 1653 to protect against Indian attacks and to keep cattle from straying. Even before the Revolutionary War, merchants, brokers, and other financial men gathered to do business in the area on and near Wall Street, in coffeehouses, and outside. By the 1830s, when the term Wall Street took on its broader meaning, many banks and commercial enterprises lined the street. A writer in 1868 described the rows of banks and insurance offices on Wall Street, with the lawyers on higher floors and the brokers in basements.

> Add to this picture innumerable groups of earnest-talking, scolding, chaffing, gesticulating men, dividing the rapid currents of merchants, brokers, clerks, foreign consuls, financiers, and commercial editors, who are continually passing, and one who has never seen the notorious thoroughfare will have a tolerably graphic idea of Wall Street.[1]

By the end of the First World War, New York had become the acknowledged world center for trading securities. Then as now, Wall Streeters were so absorbed in the stock market that, when Edwin Lefevre described a Wall Streeter in 1916, he wrote,

> He lived in the district where men do not say "Good-morning" on meeting one another, but "How's the market?" or, when one asks: "How do you feel?" receives for an answer: "Bullish!" or "Bearish!" instead of a reply regarding the state of health.[2]

Wall Street has long been simply *the Street* to those who work there, just as Exchange Alley is *the Alley* to the British. In place of the greeting "How's the market?" an American broker might ask, "What's new on the Street?" To answer that question, *The Wall Street Journal* runs the stock market column titled "Heard on the Street." Personifications of Wall Street—such as "The Street

is uneasy," or "The Street doesn't like such-and-such a stock"—
are sprinkled throughout daily conversation on the stock market.

THE BIG BOARD

In 1792, twenty-four brokers who frequently traded near a buttonwood tree in front of 68 Wall Street signed an agreement to favor
each other in trading and not to trade "any kind of Public Stocks
at a less rate than one-quarter of one percent Commission." From
this pact, known in market folklore as the **Buttonwood Tree
Agreement,** grew the New York Stock Exchange (NYSE). To
commemorate that signing on its 164th anniversary in 1956, Exchange members planted a young buttonwood tree at the entrance to the NYSE where the original tree once grew.

The New York Stock Exchange has become in time the most
powerful exchange in the world. Along the way, it harbored the
spirit of exclusiveness behind the original pact, whose signers agreed
to "give preference to each other in our Negotiations." Outsiders
resentful of the NYSE's closed doors labeled it **the Club.** Until
the 1960s, men from the upper social classes, many of them An-
glo-Saxon Protestants from Ivy League schools, dominated the
Club. Only during the 1960s did outsiders, including a few women,
begin to break the Exchange's social barriers.

Traditions, including practical jokes, initiated newcomers and
provided a bond for members, as well as mystifying or excluding
outsiders. In 1865, according to broker James Medbery, exchange
members enjoyed throwing paper darts at visiting clergymen, and
chanting "Josh, josh, josh," to wake fellow brokers who had fallen
asleep. Over one hundred years later, a similar spirit reigned. A
1969 article in *Institutional Investor* described the "youthful goings-
on," which included,

> Piles of shaving cream on Bob Meffert's shoes. Eddie Cohan's
> deadly aim with a water pistol. John Uzielli handcuffed to a
> post for two hours. . . . Buddy Conklin's shirt being ripped

off by an active crowd. Buddy Conklin's shirt being ripped off again by an active crowd.[3]

Due to heavy fines, such pranks have become less common, though traders still douse anyone about to be married with talcum powder.

The *crowd* or *trading crowd,* such as the one that ripped off Conklin's shirt, means the group of traders and floor brokers who gather around the specialist, who makes the market in a number of stocks, at a *trading post.* According to legend, the tradition of the specialist staying in one place with a crowd around him originated in 1875 at the NYSE when a broker by the name of Boyd was immobilized with a broken leg. He conducted his trading in one spot and found it worked so well that he continued the practice after his leg had healed, and others eventually followed suit.

Today, the posts fill three rooms at the Exchange, the main trading floor, the *Garage,* and the *Blue Room.* Since the Blue Room, added in 1969, has blue walls, the origin of its name is clear. Where the Garage got its name no one seems to know for sure, though some point out that in 1922, when it was added, adding garages to houses was becoming a common practice.

The NYSE's best-known nickname is the *Big Board.* In 1911, according to a glossary of stock market terms, Big Board was used in any city where two exchanges existed, to distinguish the larger from the smaller.[4] Today, however, it applies to only the NYSE, which once went by the name New York Stock and Exchange Board. "Board" on Wall Street originally referred to a board of brokers, or a stock exchange, and later to a blackboard where stock prices were listed.

THE GUTTERSNIPES

The Big Board is larger in size and volume of business than the American Stock Exchange, sometimes known as the *Little Board*— a nickname previously applied to the Consolidated Exchange in New York, which closed in 1927. The organization now known as the American Stock Exchange, or the **Amex,** once operated out-of-doors, and didn't move inside until 1921. Because the traders conducted their business on the streets, they were known as **curb-stone brokers** and the exchange, when first organized, was the New York Curb Market. Famous market trader Jesse Livermore liked to tell a version of a Wall Street anecdote, in which he refers to **curb stocks:**

> A stock trader attending a dinner party found himself seated next to a sophisticated woman, who started the conversation by asking him, "What do you think of Balzac, sir?" "Well, ma'am," he replied, "To tell you the truth, I never trade in them Curb stocks."

Even today, though the Exchange has changed its name, Wall Streeters will speak of a stock currently being traded **on the Curb** to mean traded on the Amex.

Rivalries flared up between the traders at the NYSE and the curbstone brokers even before the outdoor traders had a formal organization. In those days, no one controlled who traded in the streets, whereas the NYSE had entry requirements and a black-ball system. Three blackballs kept an applicant out, thus effectively excluding those who didn't fit the Exchange's mold. The immigrants—many of them Jews or Irishmen—stood little chance of joining the NYSE, whose members derided them by calling the curb exchange the **gutter market** and nicknaming the outside brokers **guttersnipes,** a slang term for street urchins or people of low moral character. As recently as the 1950s, one once-rejected group, the Irish, so dominated the American Stock Exchange that it was known on the Street as the **Irish-American Exchange.**

Trading out-of-doors, in summer and winter, sun and rain, and competing with the other traffic in the street made for a rough-and-tumble existence. As at the NYSE, pranks relieved the tension of heavy trading and the dullness of slow days. Around the turn of the century, traders would pour water over each other, shoot water pistols, and send new clerks with messages for Mr. Bull or Mr. Bear. In recent years, traders have still teased each other with practical jokes: dousing another's shoes with talcum powder and yelling "It's snowing in New York"; fixing paper spurs to an unsuspecting victim's shoes; clapping paper hatchets on someone's back, or signs with messages such as "Kill This Man" or "Wimp of the Month."

Such folk traditions, along with the legends traders share, unify them as a group. But, as the rivalry between exchanges shows, Wall Street is by no means one close-knit, congenial group. At various junctures within each exchange, factions have waged in-house battles. The NYSE experienced an intense power struggle in the 1930s between its *old guard,* led by exchange president Richard Whitney, and a group known as the *Elders.* An article about the internal fight, "The Battle of the Market Place," that appeared in *The Saturday Evening Post* in 1938, explained the nickname of the reform-minded group, which

> had been meeting weekly at the Luncheon Club of Wall Street, laying plans to modify the policies of the Whitney group. In tribute to their age, influence and wisdom in Wall Street's ways, the Exchange called them the Committee of Elders.[5]

At the Amex, that organization's *old guard,* the traders with the most power, came into conflict, also over the question of reform, during the late 1930s, with the so-called *young turks,* who weren't all young but were excluded from the inmost circle. Another group of young turks arose at the Amex in the early 1960s, again advocating reform. Neither old guard nor young turk is peculiar to the stock market. Old guard, which comes from the name for the imperial French guard—*Vieille Garde* in French— created by Napoleon in 1804, now means an established, influential group, typically a dominant conservative group in a political party. Young turk originally applied to a member of a revolutionary party in Turkey in the early twentieth century, and now means a member of an insurgent group, usually in a political party.

OTHER EXCHANGES, PAST AND PRESENT

Over the years, a number of exchanges have opened in New York, only to close down soon or merge with other exchanges. In 1873, William Fowler described one such exchange as the *Old Board,* relating that it opened in 1862 in a basement apartment nick-named the *Coal Hole,* to which "men of all shades and classes flocked." Also known as the Public Board and later the Open Board of Brokers, this exchange became a part of the NYSE in 1869.

The New York Gold Exchange, organized in 1864, provided a trading floor in the *Gold Room* for the *goldbugs,* a word still used to describe speculators in gold, believers in that parody of the Golden Rule, "Those with the gold make the rules." The often wild trading took place in the *Cockpit,* the space around an ob-long table. A *Harper's Weekly* article in 1869 described a surpris-ing feature in the room's decor:

> Imagine a hippotheatron, with a little fountain in the centre. The centre of the fountain is a bronze Cupid with a dolphin in its arms. From the head of Cupid arises a tiny silver stream, which falls in jets into the basin below. Fancy an iron railing ninety feet in circumference about this basin, then a space of some twenty feet between the walls and the fountain, and you have a rough idea of the Gold Room.[6]

During the mid-1800s, New Yorkers called shares traded on exchanges outside New York *foreign shares.* Many major cities, including Philadelphia, Boston, and Chicago, have been home to the so-called foreign shares, and found themselves skirmishing with New York for business. When Philadelphia brokers felt frus-trated because ships bearing news from Europe reached New York first, they ingeniously set up a system of mirrors and lights to flash the news down through New Jersey to Pennsylvania. On the op-posite coast, the San Francisco exchange opened in 1882, in such disrepute that its forty traders were known as the *forty thieves,* with each one dubbed *Ali Baba.* The Los Angeles exchange, which opened in 1899, made its home on Spring Street from 1931–85, which became known as the *Wall Street of the West.* These two California exchanges merged in 1957 to form the Pacific Coast Stock Exchange, renamed the Pacific Stock Exchange in 1973. Called the *P-Coast* or the PSE, it has trading floors in both cities.

THE LAST FRONTIER

Chicago and more specifically its La Salle Street dominate commodity trading in this country. Nevertheless, though physically centered in the Midwest, the futures markets fall under the umbrella term for all trading, *Wall Street,* making up perhaps its riskiest segment. "No one ever makes money in commodity trading; they just lend it to you till you give it back," say commodity traders, who estimate that ninety percent of those who trade in commodities lose their money and five percent break even, which leaves only five percent coming out ahead.

Wild speculation in commodities has a long and checkered history, not confined to the United States. One of its most notorious episodes still holds a place among market legends, aptly remembered as *tulipomania.* Charles Makay gave fascinating details about the madness in his 1850 book *Memoirs of Extraordinary Popular Delusions.* The story goes that in the 1630s, Europe went crazy over tulips. The flowers, newly imported from Turkey, became so popular that tulip bulbs skyrocketed in price and started a wave of speculation that swept the continent. At markets set up solely for trading tulip bulbs, stock traders started speculating in tulips, which attracted inexperienced investors from gentry to farmers, who bought bulbs hoping to sell them later at a higher price, sometimes mortgaging their homes to finance the ventures. In the whirlwind of tulipomania, an eager speculator acquired a single bulb of a rare species by paying four oxen, eight swine, twelve sheep, one thousand pounds of cheese, and a host of other items.

According to one legend, at the height of the frenzy a sailor just off the ship strode into the Amsterdam exchange—the hub of tulip trading—and, thinking he was eating an onion, consumed a tulip bulb worth the equivalent of ten thousand dollars, and soon found himself in jail. It was in Amsterdam, where the world's first stock exchange opened in 1611, that the madness and soaring prices topped out. For no obvious reason, confidence that prices would keep rising suddenly snapped, and a selling panic ensued that brought a crashing end to the tulip madness.

Though it no longer includes tulips, one area of commodities trading, called the *spot market,* involves actual physical products, and some exchange floors still have samples of wheat, corn, and other agricultural products for traders to inspect. Far more often, commodities traders deal in the futures market, buying and selling contracts for future delivery of a product and closing out the contract before taking delivery of the goods. Although everyone in the market has heard the story about a speculator who goes off on vacation, forgetting to close out a contract, and comes home to a lawn full of soybeans, it rarely occurs.

Because of its perils, commodity trading has been dubbed the *last frontier,* a label that captures the Wild West atmosphere at the Chicago Board of Trade (CBOT), the Chicago Board Options Exchange (CBOE), and the Chicago Mercantile Exchange, known as the *Merc.* New York also boasts several commodities exchanges, among them another *Merc,* the New York Mercantile Exchange; the *Comex,* the Commodity Exchange; and the *Knife,* the New York Futures Exchange.

Whereas traders at stock exchanges gather around posts to trade, commodity traders stand in *pits,* concentric circles of rising steps. Life in the pits can be hectic: hours of screaming, jockeying for position, flashing hand signals. The addition in recent years of financial futures and stock market index futures, and organized trading in options has proved so popular that those areas now dominate the futures market, surpassing the other pits in volume and near-bedlam.

Yet the nickname *The House that Bellies Built,* once attached to Chicago's Merc, indicates the original importance to the Chicago exchanges of agricultural products such as pork bellies. Maxims connected to agriculture can be heard on the exchange floors; for example, "Rain makes grain" and "Plant in dust, and your bins will bust." Traders in agricultural futures become obsessed with the weather in the hope it will help them predict the market in various crops. Some consult the meteorologists that brokerages employ, while others turn to old-fashioned folk beliefs, that predict long, cold winters when beavers' tails grow thicker than in most years and squirrels build their nests unusually high.

Like their stock market counterparts, the **pit traders** relieve tension with pranks and light-hearted pastimes, as described in a June 6, 1985, *Wall Street Journal* article about the T-Bond pit at the CBOT:

> When all else fails, the pit clowns ease the pressure with comic relief. After one trader took a routine pratfall on the steps of the pit, a clerk recalls, other traders pulled out cards like diving judges to rate his form on a scale of one to 10.

Betting on just about anything occupies spare moments— some say that the love of gambling explains why many traders in commodities and stocks are in the business. A story from the commodities pits tells of an arm wrestling contest between two employees from brokerage houses, with bets running as high as $1000, for a total pot of $70,000.

HAND SIGNALS

The distinctive non-oral language of hand signals constitutes a fascinating part of Wall Street lore. Now integrated into trading at the Amex, hand signals originated in the days of the curbstone market. When on the street, traders relied on clerks leaning out of windows or sitting on ledges of nearby buildings to relay orders that had come in. Because the clerks couldn't always be heard above the noise, they devised hand signals to convey information to the traders, who wore colorful jackets and hats so their clerks could distinguish them in the crowd. Henry Fowler commented in 1873 about the hand signals,

> A crook of the finger, a slight nod of the head, or a wink of the eye, . . . settles the business done between buyer and seller. This language of signs is as distinct and definite a part of the Wall Street lingo as that of words and figures.[7]

Unscrupulous traders found that the crooks of fingers and nods of heads invited sign stealing. If a cheating trader intercepted a signal and hurried to buy the order first, he could make a certain profit by selling it immediately to the trader for whom the signal was meant. Therefore, stealing of signs became a crime on the curb, and anyone guilty of it found himself ostracized.

The commodity exchanges also rely on hand signals. For example, in pits at the CBOE, traders who signal price and quantity also have a lexicon of amusing hand signals that stand for brokerage names. Expert in such signals are the two-dollar brokers who carry out business for more than one firm, and so need to indicate to clerks which firm they are making a trade for.

This language without words derives most of its signals from the wordplay. For example, to indicate Paine Webber, the broker rubs the back of his neck as if he had a pain there. A trade for E.F. Hutton requires making a little hut by putting together the fingers of both hands, and for Charles Schwab, making a swabbing motion as if cleaning a windshield. A simple "W" with the fingers means Dean Witter.

When the two-dollar broker mimes piercing one hand with a finger of the other hand, the clerk reads "Merrill Lynch Pierce." A shooting motion with the fingers means Shatkin, because it sounds like "shotgun," and pointing to one's head means A.G. Edwards, because "head" rhymes with "ed." The broker conveys N.K. & Co. with a knocking motion, derived from the company's initials, and Shearson Lehman with a cutting motion like a scissors, playing on the word "shears."

The Jewish stereotype of a large nose furnishes the signal for

Goldberg Brothers, whose Jewish-sounding name prompts the trader to point to his nose. From an inside joke, traders point to their chests to signal Drexel Burnham, because, they say, the women working for Drexel are so busty.

Wordplay through hand signals characterizes another exchange floor, far from Chicago. At the Tokyo Stock Exchange, traders signal stock names through a rich vocabulary of hand signals. Like their Chicago counterparts, the Japanese traders use some simple gestures; the W for Dean Witter at the CBOE corresponds to the way the Japanese indicate Victor Co. of Japan, forming a V with their fingers. They too have signals concerning women's breasts, as well as bawdier topics. An article in the December 6, 1986, *Wall Street Journal* reported about Tokyo's exchange floor:

> Sometimes they get dirty down there, flashing bawdy gestures at one another as they move billions of yen. . . . To deal in Meiji Milk Products Co., one trader signals another by pointing to his eye, or *me* (pronounced "may," like the first syllable of Meiji), then motions to his breast, for milk.

To signal the France Bed Company, a trader will lick the inside of his wrist, "suggestive of bedroom play."

OVER THE COUNTER

Before stocks in the United States were traded at exchanges, they were bought and sold at banks, where the transactions took place over a counter. Later, brokerages also did business over a counter with the customer on the other side. Thus grew the **over-the-counter** market in securities, known as the **OTC,** although, as one observer put it, "If the market were being named today it might better be called the 'over-the-telephone' market," since the physical counter has largely disappeared.

Securities that are not listed on any exchange floor are traded in the OTC market, traded **off-board.** Today, OTC traders make transactions through a computer system called NASDAQ, which stands for National Association of Securities Dealers Automated

Quotation System. Since its establishment in 1971, NASDAQ has captured an increasingly large part of the securities market, which some Wall Streeters see as a threat to the NYSE and to the role of exchange floor trading.

With increasing frequency, listed securities are traded over-the-counter in transactions that make up the **Third Market,** though definitions of the first two markets differ. Some see the issuing of new stocks and bonds by investment houses as the primary market, with the exchanges as the secondary one. More commonly on the Street, the NYSE comes first, the regional markets second, and the OTC, including the trading in listed securities, third.

BUYING A SEAT TO STAND ON THE FLOOR

Although the trading floor, the heart of stock market activity, has no chairs, a new member in an exchange purchases a *seat,* as it has been called for years. In fact, at Chicago's Merc, rules prohibit sitting on anything including garbage cans and coffee urns. As one might guess, traders at the exchanges used to sit on chairs, at a time when business was conducted by auction. Writing in 1871, James Medbery described armchairs that surrounded the sunken area where trading took place, explaining that traders jumped up out of their chairs when trading grew heated.

Wall Streeters keep an eye on the price of a seat on the NYSE, and react with sarcastic comparisons to low prices. In the mid-1970s, when a seat sold for $35,000, after having reached $515,000 in 1968, the Street noted that a McDonald's franchise "cost only four times more and was twenty times more desirable." Other humorists at the time pointed out that it cost more for a New York taxi medallion, a fact that traders recalled in April 1987 when a NYSE seat sold for the record high of $1 million.

TAPE-WORMS AND TICKER-HOUNDS

"Don't fight the tape" has echoed on Wall Street for many a year. When Wall Streeters talk about *the tape,* they mean the running list of all transactions, with their prices and volumes, that take place on the New York Stock Exchange. In the past, the list was punched out on ticker tape, a machine patented in 1867; today it usually appears on an electronic screen. (Transactions at the Amex also appear on a tape, but to market professionals "the tape" indicates the NYSE.)

Before the coming of the ticker tape, traders sent stock quotations to the brokerages written on pads of paper, carried by messengers called *pad-shovers*. When it appeared, some Wall Streeters refused to start using the ticker, and stuck to the old ways. For years, broker William Heath had dashed from exchange floor to office, shouting the prices to other brokers and earning the nickname the *Great American Reindeer*. The coming of the ticker tape didn't stop Heath, who kept up his traditional rounds.

But most Wall Streeters adjusted, and in time came to revere the tape, imbuing it with a personality of its own. "The tape never lies" joined the stock market proverb, apparently borrowed from card players who contend that, "The cards never lie." "I never argue with the tape," a trader might say, or when a stock's price changes drastically, "the tape is screaming" about it.

Because speculators believe that *watching the tape* gives a feel for the market or a particular stock, many on the Street are dedicated *tape-watchers*. Wall Streeters used to call these watchers *tape-worms*, hinting that an addiction to the tape could devour the speculator.

The unhealthy nature of the ticker tape emerged again in two humorous terms in Wall Street lingo. Glossaries in 1903, 1911, and 1953 list *tickerosis*, "for the mania of a speculator to hang over the ticker," with the 1953 list giving as a synonym, *tickeritis*.[8] In the 1920s, traders spoke of *ticker-hounds*, whose addiction to the tape as often as not didn't pay off, and *ticker-sense*, a keenly developed skill in the market that did pay.

So closely linked has the ticker tape been to Wall Street that traders in the past have called the Street the *Lane of the Ticker*, the *Street of Ticker Tape*, and *Ticker Tape Stem*.

THE SCENE UPSTAIRS

The tape conveys the Exchange activities to another main component of Wall Street, the brokerages, often referred to as *houses.* While those who trade at the exchange are *on the floor,* the retail brokers that most customers deal with reside *upstairs,* even if their offices are on the ground floor. In fact, for all the publicity that the exchange floors get, the bulk of Wall Streeters work upstairs, where they have come up with slang to describe their surroundings.

Although they won't see pitchers warming up, visitors to a brokerage may see its *bull pen,* an open space where retail brokers sit at desks and spend their days telephoning prospective clients, *dialing for dollars,* an expression borrowed from a television game show. The *back office,* on the other hand, consists of the departments not directly concerned with sales or trading. In the second half of the 1960s, when the market was booming, the back office became the center of attention when brokerages couldn't keep up with their paperwork, a crisis known as *back-office crunch.* An unusually large number of *fails* occurred, failures to deliver certificates or to complete transactions in the designated time, along with many *aged fails,* those thirty or more days late. The NYSE responded to the crisis by closing on Wednesdays for several months, and shortening hours temporarily.

One part of the back office is the *cage,* the brokerage's cashier division, named in the days when cashiers stood behind bars. Massive work at the end of a frenzied trading day brings about *rage in the cage,* an explosion of paperwork—and sometimes of tempers.

An invisible barrier, dubbed a *Chinese Wall,* is erected wherever communication between departments is formally forbidden. Since mergers and acquisition specialists are barred from discussing their dealings with the retail and trading personnel, the firm must construct a Chinese Wall between them, to prevent exchange of inside information. Ideally, invisible walls also separate research and underwriting. But as recent cases of insider trading have revealed, financial Chinese Walls are far less substantial than the Great Wall of China, from which they take their name.

To promote communication, the big brokerages create a network between their home offices and branch offices throughout the country, using the *squawk box.* This two-way cable radio features up-to-the minute news of world events, interviews with floor traders and analysts, and—given top billing—promotions of products the brokerage wants to push. Although some firms, such as the small *boutiques* that offer specialized service, have no need for squawk boxes, they are indispensable to the firms at the other end of the scale, which also take their nickname from retail shopping, the *financial supermarkets.* These brokerages offer their customers a wide range of financial products, including stocks, bonds, options, tax shelters, futures contracts, various indexes, and other investments, a range described by Wall Street wits as covering *from womb to tomb.*

SOLLY, OPCO, AND CHURCHYARD & GRAVES

Wall Streeters like to bestow slang names on brokerage firms, just as they nickname stocks and colleagues, and no firm has received more than Merrill Lynch, the biggest of the financial supermarkets. From the first, the company's founder Charles Merrill aspired to build *The Department Store of Finance,* a phrase that has become a nickname for the firm. Its large number of clients and brokers inspire the other names, such as *The Thundering Herd, The Bureau of Missing Persons* and, from the first three words of the Constitution of the U.S., *We, the People,* a nickname for more than thirty years. *The Wall Street Journal* reported on April 14, 1983, about the firm's use of one of its nicknames:

> Merrill originally used the bull as a symbol of "the thundering herd," the nickname for the firm. When strategists decided that this insulted both brokers and investors by suggesting that they merely followed the crowd, Merrill brought in a new ad agency.

The bull stayed on to convey the opposite message—the current "breed apart" campaign.

Wall Streeters also call Merrill Lynch *Big Blue,* borrowed from a nickname for the stock of IBM, perhaps because both, in their own ways, play dominant roles in the market.

Before it merged into other firms, CBWL—Cogan, Berlind, Weill & Levitt—was known on the Street as *Corned Beef with Lettuce.* Equally harmless, though less clever, are a number of other nicknames, such as *Goldy* or *Goldman Slacks* for Goldman, Sachs, *Solly* for Salomon Brothers, *Pru Bache* for Prudential Bache, and *Opco* for Oppenheimer & Company. *FOB* for First Boston dates back to when it was First National Bank of Boston, several decades ago.

Jokers like to call Kidder Peabody, *Kidder Nobody,* but more often it's simply *KP.* But not all the nicknames are so mild. While Shearson Lehman/American Express sometimes goes by *Slamex,* those close to it also call Shearson, affectionately or not, the *Slob.* When discount brokers, known as *disco brokers,* started offering lower commissions in return for less advice, their full-service rivals sought verbal revenge. Thus, Quick & Reilly was dubbed *Quick & Dirty,* and Charles Schwab *Cheapo Charlie.* More insulting still, traders twist the name of Blinder, Robinson & Co., a firm that specializes in penny stocks, into *Blind 'em and Rob 'em,* because of its run-ins with the SEC.

The insider trading scandals of the 1980s opened Drexel Burnham Lambert up for its share of ridicule on Wall Street. Because Dennis Levine of that firm kept his profits from illegal dealings in a bank in the Bahamas, jokes sprang up that poked fun at Drexel, such as this one:

> Shearson Lehman Brothers' latest slogan is "Minds over Money," and Smith Barney's is "We Make Money the Old-Fashioned Way." What is Drexel Burnham's? "It's better in the Bahamas."

Even before the scandals, Drexel provoked controversy by advancing the use of junk bonds for hostile takeovers. When the firm started to promote this takeover technique at an annual seminar, onlookers nicknamed the event **the predators' ball.** They joked that, because it attracted so many key raiders, arbs, and takeover lawyers, if a disgruntled executive whose company had been preyed upon set off a bomb at the ball, it would effectively wipe out the hostile takeover movement.

Another company's slogan that has suffered at the hands of parodists, Smith Barney's "We make money the old-fashioned way: We earn it" was inevitably altered to "We make money the old-fashioned way: We churn it."

Not content just to play with the real firm names, Wall Street wits have also created facetious brokerage houses over the years, being careful to make the names sound like the real thing. As early as 1871, James Medbery wrote about the firm of **Takem & Makem,** since traders then yelled "take 'em" to bid for a stock.[9] At the exchanges today, a floor broker in a jovial mood will answer the telephone announcing the off-color firm name of **Lay Back & Whack It** or the more sedate one of **Churchyard & Graves.**

THE WATCHDOG ON WALL STREET

The Securities and Exchange Commission, though it is based in Washington, D.C., and not in Manhattan, effectively resides in Wall Street, dubbed by slang as the **Watchdog on Wall Street.** When the Senate created it in 1934 in response to the crash of 1929 and its devastating wake, Will Rogers explained, "The senate passed a bill to regulate Wall Street. The government is going to put traffic lights on it; it's always been a hit-and-run street."

President Roosevelt had some explaining to do when he appointed the first head of the SEC, Joseph Kennedy, who himself had a questionable reputation as a stock market speculator. FDR justified his appointment with an allusion to "Set a thief to catch a thief." Not many years later, when William O. Douglas became SEC chairman, he used a phrase with a similar cadence to explain, privately, why he wanted to enlist the help of the NYSE in preventing market rigging. "You need a snoop to catch a jiggle," Douglas said, borrowing the slang term *jiggle* from Wall Street, where it meant a minor market manipulation.

The SEC has engendered some of its own slang terms over the years. In the 1950s, SEC investigators scoffed at brokerages as *funeral parlors.* Today when the agency examines a preliminary registration statement from a company that plans to issue securities, if the statement proves deficient, the SEC sends the company a *bedbug letter,* telling them what bugs to take out. The agency subscribes to the *shingle theory,* a theory shared by the legal profession, that implies that when a brokerage opens for business by "hanging out a shingle," the new firm implicitly agrees to deal honestly with clients.

Before the SEC, *blue sky laws,* a term first recorded in 1912, offered the main government action against investment fraud. These laws, enacted in different forms by various states, aimed at preventing companies from selling stock that had the value of "a patch of blue sky" and nothing else. When a stock has been duly registered in a state, which includes disclosing financial information, it has been *blue-skied.*

The creation of the SEC introduced a national scale into investment regulation, focusing it on Wall Street. Because the Amex entrance is on Broad Street, the agency gained the nickname *Policeman at the Corner of Wall and Broad.* At times, advocates of strict regulation have complained that the SEC does indeed behave like the policeman on the corner—"never there when you need help." They have charged that Wall Street's white collar crime, even when detected, carried little punishment.

But to the satisfaction of those advocates, the 1980s found the policeman walking his beat with renewed vigilance. When John Shad took over as chairman of the SEC in 1981, he vowed to "come down on insider trading with hobnail boots," and has done just that. In the SEC's current war on Wall Street crime, offenders don't walk away from convictions with just the punishment of never working in the brokerage world again. Prison terms and heavy fines are the order of the day, and this old Wall Street joke no longer rings true:

Two clerks from a big Wall Street firm were wheeling a cart filled with negotiable bonds worth $4 million from one office to another. The younger clerk wanted to grab the bonds, make a getaway, and live happily ever after. "I'm an Irish citizen," he said. "They can't extradite me." The other clerk, who had worked so many years on Wall Street that he was long past retirement age, looked horrified. "Do you realize what would happen if we were caught?" he said. "What?" asked the younger man. "Why," came the answer, "we could never work on Wall Street again."

9

Blue Mondays and Black Fridays: Nicknames of Events and Times

*October, this is one of the peculiarly dangerous months to spec-
ulate in stocks. The others are: July, January, September, April,
November, May, March, June, December, August, and February.*

Fortunately for the stock market, Mark Twain's warning has not
been heeded. Yet Wall Street's own slang suggests that not only
months but days, years, and eras have imperiled investors
throughout the history of speculating. Eras and events which
brought happiness to investors are also recorded, though in fewer
numbers.

BLACK AND BLUE MONDAYS

According to market superstitions, individual days of the week are
the most dangerous periods. The most prevalent advice concerning weekdays is "Never buy stock on Friday," because bad news

can break over the weekend, leading to plunging prices on Monday. As they say on Wall Street, "All wars and devaluations start on weekends." When a disaster hits, speculators cannot sell immediately because the markets are closed on Saturday and Sunday. If the news is bad enough, during the two days without trading, panic sets in and grows. For example, the SEC chose Friday afternoon after the markets had closed on November 14, 1986, to announce Ivan Boesky's guilty plea to insider trading and his agreement to cooperate with the authorities. After a weekend of increasing tension, the market dropped fifty-six points on Monday and Tuesday combined.

When the weekend leads to a turbulent Monday, or when trading is sluggish—as it often is on Monday—Wall Streeters complain about a **Blue Monday.** A series of subsequent bad Mondays lead to complaints about a **Blue Monday syndrome.** A day calamitous enough to go down in stock market history becomes *the* Blue Monday of that time. Not an expression peculiar to the stock market, Blue Monday in the Middle Ages was the Monday before Lent, because—according to one theory—after a weekend of pre-Lenten drunken revels, everyone felt blue from their hangovers. Another folk etymology explains that churches were decorated in blue that day, while in a third theory Blue Monday comes from a custom of flogging errant sailors on Monday, which turned them black and blue.

On Wall Street, investors turn figuratively black and blue on Blue Mondays, beaten by a merciless market or fellow traders. "That was a blue Monday for the ursine tribe," wrote William Fowler about a day in 1864 when bulls were crushing the bears.[1]

In 1928, the San Francisco Stock Exchange suffered a major decline on June 11th, and the next day, *The New York Times* reported,

> "Blue Monday," a term which probably will be applied to this day in California Stock Market history, saw the greatest break that ever took place in Western stock prices. . . . An amazed public saw Bank of Italy break 160 points, Bancitaly drop 86

points, Bank of America descend 120 points and United Security 80 points.

Another market slump remembered as Blue Monday occurred on May 28, 1962. After declining for several weeks, the market reached a low point that Monday, when the Dow Jones Industrial Average (DJIA) fell 34.95 points, the biggest plunge since 1929. Trading became so wild that the ticker tape ran up to sixty-nine minutes late, in turn intensifying the sense of panic. Another Blue Monday took its place in Wall Street history on November 21, 1966, when cutbacks and announcements over the weekend of losses in the automobile industry sent the market plummeting.

A recent Monday has made its mark indelibly on the market: **Black Monday,** October 19, 1987, when the Dow dropped 508 points and trading volume at the NYSE topped 604 million shares, almost double the previous volume record. The crash, as some called it, stunned Wall Street and the country. Stocks had already posted a record loss the preceding Friday, dropping 108.36 points. Those who believed that Friday served as the major correction for the five-year bull market were proved wrong on Monday.

In the days that followed Black Monday, the market resembled a violent roller-coaster ride, not just in the United States, but on exchanges throughout the world. The Dow gained on Tuesday, and mounted its largest single-day climb ever on Wednesday, up 186.84 points, all in overwhelmingly heavy and volatile trading. The following Monday, the market plunged again, in its second biggest loss in history. Meanwhile, markets in Tokyo, London, and elsewhere experienced unprecedented losses and gains.

After a period of shock, Wall Street regained its sense of humor and started generating jokes about the catastrophe. Those who blamed it on the lack of leadership from President Reagan's White House quipped that "The crash wouldn't have happened if Reagan was still president." Other jokes revealed resentment against Wall Street yuppies and their exorbitant incomes:

What's the difference between a 28-year-old arb and a pigeon?

A pigeon can still make a deposit on a Porsche.

What do you call a young broker in suspenders?
Hey, waiter!

How many investment bankers fit in the back of a pickup truck?
Two, with their lawnmowers.

WALL STREET LAYS AN EGG ON TUESDAY

Although fewer disasters seem to occur on Tuesdays than on other days of the week, when **Black Tuesday** of October 29, 1929, erupted, it brought more anguish to investors than any other day in previous market history. It was the climax of the **Crash of 1929,** but not the first sign of the fall—the stock market had tumbled in June 1928, December 1928, and March 1929, only to recover again, at least in certain stocks.

Even during the previous month, the market had fallen steeply in an event called the **Babson Break,** on September 5, 1929, a Thursday. When a stock analyst named Roger Babson predicted—on a slow news day—that stocks were due for a collapse, the prediction made headlines. It became self-fulfilling when, the next day, a storm broke on the market and prices plunged, wiping out hundreds of small speculators.

The market recovered temporarily until the crash late the next month, which culminated in Black Tuesday's devastation. As prices fell, more than sixteen million shares traded hands, far more than the previous record for one day. The next day's edition of *Varsity* summed up the catastrophe in the famous irreverent headline: "Wall Street Lays an Egg."

BLACK WEDNESDAYS

One **Black Wednesday** cast its gloom on July 26, 1893, the low point of a persistent bear market, a day when many stocks reached their nadir for the year. On the previous day, the Erie Railroad had gone into bankruptcy—one of the numerous railroad failures that year—prompting the collapse on Wednesday and during the following two weeks. Looking back in 1894, Louis Windmuller wrote in *Harper's Weekly*, "During the summer the tension became so great that men who had to weather the financial storm almost sank under the weight of business cares to their graves."[2]

Better remembered is the **Black Wednesday** of October 23, 1929 that preceded Black Tuesday. The last hour of trading saw 2,600,000 shares sold at decreasing prices, with the ticker tape running far behind. Commenting the next day, Will Rogers called Black Wednesday a "wailing day":

> When Wall Street took that tail spin, you had to stand in line
> to get a window to jump out of, and speculators were selling
> space for bodies in the East River.[3]

THURSDAY'S CYCLONES

In describing John "Bet-A-Million" Gates, Bernard Baruch wrote of his reaction to the panic on **Black Thursday**, May 9, 1901:

> "What do you think of the flurry, Mr. Gates?" he was asked.
> "Flurry?" he retorted. "If you call that a flurry, I never want
> to be in a cyclone."
> "Are you broke?" someone asked impertinently.
> "Just badly bent," retorted the game old warhorse.[4]

Black Thursday resulted from the panic in Northern Pacific stock, nicknamed **Nipper.** Numerous small investors, drawn into the market by dreams of sudden wealth, had sold Nipper stock short. The cyclone hit them on May 9th when the price of Nipper skyrocketed, while other stock prices collapsed. Northern Pacific rose to $1000 per share, though by late in the day it had fallen to $300.

In reporting the widespread losses, *The Commercial & Financial Chronicle* described the collapse as "the most extraordinary incident in Wall Street history," and predicted that speculators would learn a lesson from it:

The mania of the public, we imagine, will hardly be renewed on an equal scale. The outsider is likely to be most impressed by the fact that the spell was broken, that there are unexpected and serious dangers in the most promising speculation, and that belief in the invulnerability of any such movement is therefore a delusion.

But October 24, 1929, inevitably dubbed **Black Thursday,** showed how wrong the *Chronicle* was in its prediction. The Great Bull Market of the 1920s had cast a spell of immense proportions and when the spell was broken, speculators were overwhelmed with fear. Thursday topped the day before in tragedy; 12,894,650 shares traded hands, dropping in price all the while. It marked the undeniable end to the bull market and became the first big day of the Crash, when the bottom dropped out of the market.

But meanwhile, at the offices of J.P. Morgan and Company, the powerful of Wall Street were meeting to try to thwart the crash. Word of the meeting started to buoy up the market, and when Exchange vice-president Richard Whitney walked—some say ran—across the floor at 1:30, as an envoy from the meeting, and confidently called out a bid for U.S. Steel, a short-lived recovery set in. But by Black Tuesday, confidence had disappeared and the Crash continued.

THURSDAYS BLOODY AND SILVER

The street outside of the offices of J.P. Morgan and Company, at which the Black Thursday meeting took place, was the setting for an earlier tragedy, on September 16, 1920, known in market folklore as **Bloody Thursday.** On that day, a bomb exploded in Wall Street near the corner of Wall and Broad, shaking the ground and blowing windows in. At the Stock Exchange, glass hurtled onto the floor but, luckily for the traders, the building's glass dome did not fall.

On the street not far from the explosion, the members of the New York Curb Exchange, who were trading outdoors, found themselves in the midst of chaos. The bomb killed thirty people instantly; three hundred people suffered injuries, from which ten of them later died. Popular sentiment pinned the crime on "Reds," but the mystery of who set off the bomb was never solved.

Silver Thursday was, figuratively speaking, another bloody day on the Street, due to the actions of millionaire Nelson Bunker Hunt. Hunt and his brother W. Herbert Hunt had been speculating in silver futures for several years and accumulating a hoard of silver bullion. When the Hunts' buying drove up the price of silver, rumors spread that they were trying to corner the market. In 1979, Hunt persuaded Arab investors to join him in buying silver contracts, and their actions pushed the price up from $16 an ounce to a high of around $50.

But silver prices began to slip, and margin calls went out to the Hunts, including one for more than $100 million from Bache Halsey Stuart Shield, their principal silver broker. The Hunts could not meet all the calls, which had such serious implications for their brokers that on Thursday, March 27, 1980, the NYSE suspended trading in the stock of Bache and the firm of Shearson Loeb Rhoades. The news sent the Dow plunging to a five-year low in ninety minutes. By the end of the day, trading had picked up, based on reassuring statements from Shearson and Bache, but the market still closed with half the companies listed on the NYSE at their lowest price in a year.

REPEATEDLY BLACK FRIDAY

Because tragedy in the market strikes most often on Friday, Wall Street history records many *Black Fridays,* a phrase borrowed from the British, who have used it for financially or politically disastrous Fridays. According to slang expert Stuart Flexner, the expression Black Friday goes back to its role as a British synonym for Good Friday when clergymen wore black vestments. Good Friday and Black Friday are still associated in the minds of Wall Streeters, as an article in *Barron's* observed:

One story believed by many traders is that the markets close for Good Friday because the last time they stayed open on that day it became known as "Black Friday." The NYSE says that is nonsense, that the Black Friday people have in mind was a gold panic on September 24, 1869, which was nowhere near Easter. The NYSE, for the record, started celebrating the holiday in 1864.

Market operators Jay Gould and Jim Fisk brought about the Black Friday of 1869 when they attempted a corner on gold, a scheme that included bribing the brother-in-law of President Grant in hopes of influencing government policy on gold. Gould and Fisk pushed up the price of gold, which many bears had sold short, by sending their agent Albert Speyers to the floor of the Gold Room to constantly buy. He raised it to 160, but then the corner broke and, according to William Fowler,

> The bear-hammers seemed to have been all welded into one great sledge, which fell upon the price like a forty-ton boulder, and smashed it down to 135, while Speyers fell back into the crowd, quivering like an aspen. Lights seemed to dance before the eyes of the multitude, and then go out in darkness, as they rushed tumultuously into Broad Street.[5]

Fowler reported on several other Black Fridays, which occurred in the year 1873, as part of a stock market panic: September 19, October 31, and "the blackest Friday of all" three, November 7th. Next in the historical list comes Industrial Black Friday, May 5, 1893. Because a number of companies had already declared insolvency recently, when the Cordage Company failed in early May, holders of industrial stocks embarked on a selling spree, which reached its worst point on May 5th.

The wheat pit in Chicago has also been the scene of a Black Friday, on April 3, 1925. Earl Sparling, in his 1930 book *Mystery Men of Wall Street*, describes how Jesse Livermore turned this tragedy for others into profit for himself. He had started buying wheat at about one dollar per bushel and held on to it until the price reached two dollars. Then, getting out just as wheat started to slip, he turned from bull to bear, and started to sell short, profiting to the tune of several million dollars.

More recently, the Vancouver Stock Exchange suffered a Black Friday in Canada's penny stock market on October 19th, 1984, when thirty million dollars in losses were recorded. During the preceding eleven months, speculators—or market manipulators, some say—had bid up the price of six stocks, most notably Beauford Resources Ltd., far beyond their real value. On that Friday, when rumors began to circulate that the major investors were unloading those stocks, the market in them crashed, bringing other stocks down with it.

WILD AND WITCHING

Not all Fridays have been painted black by slang. Wall Streeters called Friday, January 23, 1987, **Wild Friday** because of its stunning effect on the stock, futures, and options markets. The stock market took a crazy roller-coast ride that day, when the Dow rose sixty points, then plummeted 114 points in less than an hour. In the Chicago pits, the market's volatile swing jolted traders who deal in stock market index futures and options on those futures, instruments based on the stock market's performance. Program trading—computerized tracking and trading of indexes by big institutions seeking to profit on spreads—received the blame for Wild Friday, but then was also given credit two days later when the Dow zoomed to a record high.

The other Friday not labeled black is a recurring one, dubbed **Expiration Friday,** the third Friday of the last month of each quarter. The day's fame stems from its last hour every quarter, the **triple witching hour** from 3 P.M. until the market closes at 4 P.M. At the end of that hour on every Expiration Friday, contracts are due to expire on three trading instruments: individual stock options, stock market index futures, and options on the index futures.

While the "triple" is derived from the three instruments, the "witching" comes from the strange effect the hour has on the stock, futures, and options markets, typically sending them into violent swings. For example, during the triple witching hour of March 21, 1986, stock market prices plunged, trading volume ballooned, and the tape that records trades took thirty minutes to finish after the closing bell. A year later, in contrast to most Expiration Fridays, the market's explosive trading sent the Dow up 33.95 points, pushing it past the 2300 mark for the first time, and setting a record for the eighth-busiest day in NYSE history.

In trying to subdue the bewitchment, the exchanges and regulatory agencies have come up with guidelines for Expiration Friday. Traders dubbed one rule, put into effect in June 1987, the *double triple witching hour.* It required settlement of certain stock market index futures and index options in the morning on Friday, with the others to close as usual. Under the new rules, the next Expiration Friday was indeed quiet, without the frenzy of previous triple witching hours, leading traders—perhaps prematurely—to sing out a line from *The Wizard of Oz,* "Ding dong the witch is dead."

ONE BLACK SATURDAY AND
TWO OCTOBER MASSACRES

Although the exchanges discontinued trading on Saturdays in 1952, one Saturday since then has gone down in Wall Street history. On *Black Saturday,* October 6, 1979, the Federal Reserve Board announced a new anti-inflationary monetary policy that would focus on controlling money supply rather than manipulating interest rates. When the market opened the following Monday, it started its worst slump in six years, leading Wall Streeters to label the entire month the *October Massacre.*

The previous October had also earned the name October Massacre because of a market plunge. In a poem titled "Elegy for the Bull Market (Or Bear Trap, as, with Hindsight, It Now Seems to Have Been)," Andrew Tobias viewed the 1978 debacle in hind-

sight. Two of the verses describe the progress with a note of re-
gretful humor:

> The massacre started
> The ides of October.
> The mood on the Street
> Turned suddenly sober.
>
> Then somber, then grim,
> Then grimmer, then bleak!
> Touts who'd been shouting
> Could now barely speak.[6]

THE MARKET'S MAY DAY

The best-known date in Wall Street history to take its name from
a month was **May Day,** May 1, 1975. At ten o'clock that Thursday morning, the stock brokerages entered a new era, when the
SEC forced them to end their practice of a fixed-commission and
begin negotiating fees with their customers. Wall Street, for the
most part, had resisted this revolutionary change to bring about
competitive commissions, a fear indicated by the nickname
"Mayday," the international radio distress call, derived from the
French "m'aidez," meaning "help me." But the disaster predicted
never materialized and by 1985 the president of the NYSE proclaimed that May Day was "the best thing that ever happened for
the industry."

London's equivalent of Wall Street's May Day took place on
October 27, 1986, when fixed commissions on debt and equity
dealings were eliminated and a host of new regulations went into
effect. The **Big Bang** they called it, probably derived from the
"Big Bang Theory" that contends the universe was created by an
explosion. To the London brokers, the changes promised to create a new, explosive world in place of the old one. France decided to follow suit, planning to change its stock market regulations to a lesser degree in 1988, a plan dubbed **Le Petit Bang.**

SEASONAL SWINGS

Wall Streeters try to discern patterns in the ups and downs of months in market history, and use these patterns to predict the future. For example, they say, "The bears have Thanksgiving, but the bulls have Christmas." This adage predicts a market correction in late October and November, with a year-end rally later when institutional investors dress up their portfolios for the end of the quarter. Despite the saying, since 1945, stock prices have fallen only seven times on the day after Thanksgiving and risen thirty-four times, a price rise which some Wall Streeters attribute to the feeling of geniality that comes from a good Thanksgiving celebration.

If the year-end rally does not materialize, investors can expect the following year to be a poor one in the market, a prediction put in a couplet by one Wall Streeter:

> *If Santa Claus should fail to call,*
> *Bears may come to Broad and Wall.*

Another proverb connected with holidays advises, "Sell before Rosh Hashanah and buy back at Yom Kippur." Presumably stocks don't do much on either of the days because, according to the lore, so many of the traders are in temple.

Wall Streeters also speak of the *January effect,* a tendency in the market to sell securities in November and December, to take gains for tax purposes and reestablish positions in January. As early as 1906, *Moody's Magazine* took note of the traditional Wall Street belief that stocks went down in November and December, up in January. But, the writer contended, January actually had more lows than highs, and more often trapped innocent investors:

> This seems to be a season of the year when the unexpected frequently happens, and when yaps are trimmed with great regularity.[7]

PRESIDENTIAL MARKETS

Wall Streeters name periods of prosperity in the stock market—some long, some short—after the current President. For example, the *McKinley Market* was inspired by the reelection of the popular president in November 1900. In 1901, the bull market already underway caught the fancy of many small speculators, who saw a chance to get rich quickly. On April 30, 1901, the NYSE had its first three-million-share day. Despite the setbacks of Black Thursday in May of 1901, the bull market survived and was still on course when McKinley was assassinated in September 1901.

The *Coolidge Boom* began just after the election of Calvin Coolidge in November 1923, and continued until he left office—a significant portion of the Great Bull Market of the 1920s. During the boom, speculators caught *Radio Fever,* when the stock of RCA, nicknamed Radio, experienced an enormous run-up over several years. After the Coolidge Boom came the *Hoover Bull Market,* beginning in 1928. According to *Literary Digest,*

> The "Hoover Market" got off to a flying start on the very day after election, for as one financial writer observes, "within twenty-four hours of the election the words 'Hoover market' had been substituted for 'Coolidge market' in the language of Wall Street, and predictions were being made of prosperity and an era of speculation as great under the new Administration as in that of the old."[8]

Such was the enthusiasm on Wall Street that the Monday after the election, the NYSE had its biggest day in volume up to that time, with rising prices. A cartoon titled "The Golden Stairs" that appeared with the *Literary Digest* article showed a ticker tape machine, labeled "Stock Market," dancing up stairs labeled "GOP Victory." The spirit of excitement did not foresee the Crash of 1929 or the years of depression ahead.

THE EISENHOWER MARKETS

The next substantial period of optimism in the stock market was named after President Eisenhower: the *Eisenhower Bull Market* or the *Eisenhower Boom.* In his book *N.Y.S.E.*, historian Robert Sobel explained that the boom actually began in mid-1949 during Truman's second term, but because Truman was so unpopular, Eisenhower got credit in the market's nickname.

Another market event named after President Eisenhower took place in 1955, when news about the President's illness caused the *Heart Attack Market.* Eisenhower's heart attack on Saturday, September 24th, prompted a sell-off in the market the following Monday. Once again those who advise selling on Fridays found themselves justified, as sell orders poured in on Saturday and Sunday. The Dow dropped 31.89 points, the biggest drop since October 28, 1929, and the market continued to decline for more than two weeks.

The Eisenhower era also hosted the *Sputnik Market* in the last quarter of 1957. After the Russians launched the satellite Sputnik I into outer space on October 4, 1957, the stock market became enamored of missile stocks. While the rest of the market was generally declining, stock in any corporation connected to missiles climbed in price. Between October and the following January, Douglas Aircraft stock rose twenty-six percent, General Dynamics thirty-nine percent, and Lockheed Aircraft thirty-five percent. As one Wall Streeter explained the excitement, "When you're investing in missiles, you're investing in the Space Age."

KENNEDY AND JOHNSON BULL MARKETS

When John F. Kennedy was elected in 1960, the country celebrated financially. The market began to rise steadily, and volume continually increased in a *Kennedy Bull Market.* The year of 1961 was yet another period when it seemed as though everyone was getting into the market. More shares were traded at the New York Stock Exchange than in any year since 1929—and Wall

Street praised President Kennedy. But by the next year, the honeymoon was over, and the market collapsed, reaching its low point on the Blue Monday of May 1962.

On the Friday that President Kennedy was assassinated, November 22, 1963, the stock market reacted with temporary panic, but recovered the following Tuesday, after being closed Monday to observe mourning. On the Tuesday, optimism about a Johnson administration and news about the resolution of a financial crisis at Ira Haupt & Co. inspired the single largest one-day leap in the Dow up to that time, 32.03 points. By 1963, Wall Street was talking about the **Johnson Bull Market,** which reached its peak in 1966, with the Dow cresting at 1001, its highest point of the decade. The bull market continued, off and on, through the go-go years of 1966–68, bringing wildly busy days to the Exchange floors and brokerages around the country.

WINCHELL, DARVAS, AND JOE GRANVILLE

Presidents are not the only people to inspire nicknames for stock market events; the spoken or written word of a less important man occasionally puts its mark on Wall Street history. In one case, the Sunday radio-television broadcasts of Walter Winchell, with tips about stocks, created a spurt of speculation in early 1954 dubbed the **Winchell Market.** Wall Street was not impressed with the phenomenon since stocks would rise in price immediately after the broadcast only to fall again when excitement died down.

Another outsider who gathered a crowd of followers was the Latin dancer, Nicolas Darvas, with his extravagantly titled book *How I Made $2,000,000 in the Stock Market.* His method of using stop-loss orders and his claims of success incited his readers to speculate in the market, bringing about the **Darvas Boom** in 1959.

Still fresh in the minds of investors, **Joe Granville Day** took place on January 7, 1981. When Florida seminar speaker and newsletter writer Joe Granville sent out a sell-everything signal to certain of his subscribers, who as members of the "Early Warning

System" received exclusive telephone messages, the news of his warning sent the stock market reeling. The Dow dropped twenty-three points and the market recorded $45 billion in losses, with a record set for trading volume.

PANICS

"In Wall Street a panic is a time of great alarm when there is a rush to sell securities with a ruthless sacrifice of values," wrote Howard Smith in his 1903 stock-market dictionary.[9] The word *panic* is derived from Pan, the Greek god who put fear into the hearts of humans and caused them to flee. Such uncontrollable fears periodically seize the stock market, brought about by weakness in the market or by some outside event or actor.

Stock market panics have taken their names from certain men, from stock names and nicknames such as Nipper, from years, and from an assortment of other sources. Of those named for men, the **Morse Panic** of April 1864 resulted from Anthony Morse and his colleagues's becoming overextended in the market; the **Jay Cooke Panic** of September 1873 began when Jay Cooke & Company was forced to close its doors; and the **Grant & Ward Panic** of 1884 occurred when that firm, with former President Ulysses A. Grant as a partner, announced its failure. Reversing the normal order, one fictional man has taken his name from the stock market panics instead of giving it: William Faulkner's character Wallstreet Panic Snope.

A collapse of the economy and the market in 1857, dubbed the **Banker's Panic,** also took the name **Western Blizzard,** because the country viewed it as a chilling and destructive financial storm. The panic, touched off by the failure of the Ohio Life Insurance Company, paralyzed business all over the country for more than six months.

Daniel Drew saw the calamity as a turning point in Wall Street conduct, and wrote in 1857,

> With this panic year of which I am now writing a new state of affairs came about in financial circles. The panic . . . put old

fogeyism out of date forevermore. The men who conducted business in the old-fashioned slow-poke method—the think-of-the-other fellow method—were swept away by this panic, or at least so crippled that they didn't figure much in the world of affairs afterwards.

Although most panics affect a wide range of people, two panics that took place in 1903 and 1907 were said to ruin primarily wealthy investors. These events fell into the Wall Street category of *rich man's panic,* a panic resulting from wealthy speculators rushing to sell, and suffering large losses in the process.

The fictional Mr. Dooley gave his views on panics in 1910:

> No, sir, ye can bet it ain't th' people that have no money that causes panics. Panics are th' result iv too manny people havin' money. . . . Panics an' circuses, as Father Kelly says, are f'r th' amusement iv th' poor.[10]

But no one, rich or poor, was amused by the *Panic of 1929,* also known as the *Great Crash,* which encompassed the Black Wednesday, Black Thursday, and Black Tuesday of that October. The Panic of 1929, leading as it did to the Great Depression of the 1930s, was the darkest and most memorable event in Wall Street history.

10

Inflated Images and Underlying Doubts: Analysis of Metaphors

In the vivid picture of their world that Wall Streeters paint through slang, certain patterns emerge that reveal how Wall Streeters view themselves, their activities, the public and—that uncontrollable force—the market. Metaphors of dominance, violence, sex, gambling, and uncleanliness occur again and again. Most of the comparisons drawn inflate the egos of Wall Streeters, depicting their masculine world as more macho than it truly is, but at the same time, the metaphors point to guilt feelings about work on Wall Street, its association with gambling, and its central focus, money.

Dominance—physical, sexual, even political—is a major theme in the metaphors. Regardless of whether a Wall Streeter is trying to dominate the market, fellow traders, or customers, the images of dominance exaggerate the consequences. Financial loss is equated with violent death, competition is equated with war. The slang adds figurative bludgeoning and blood to an existence filled with paper and computers, an existence which has little physical violence. By using hyperbole—the figure of speech that exaggerates—Wall Streeters depict their world as filled with life-and-death struggles, inflating its importance and therefore their own.

Images of political conquest of the market were strongest around the turn of the century, when Napoleons, Kings, and Titans frequented Wall Street. Although some of them did wield more power than anyone does today, the slang exaggerated their dominance. The Wall Street adage "No person is bigger than the market" rang as true then as it does now, judging from how many great market figures fell from glory.

Images of physical conquest also depict Wall Streeters trying to prove that they are bigger than the market. They *hammer* it, *jackscrew* it, *dump stocks* on it, and try to *saddle* it. Always trying to make a *killing* in the market, they *pound* stocks and *slaughter* them. *Eighth chasers* do their *scalping* on exchange floors, brokers *fill or kill* orders and *hit bids,* and options traders execute *strangles. Gunslingers* and *hipshooters* in the 1960s pitted themselves against the greater force of the stock market and eventually lost.

According to the language, Wall Streeters face a humbling, uphill struggle against a bloodthirsty market which fights back. The market inflicts Wall Streeters with its peculiar illnesses: *tickerosis, new-issue fever, merger mania.* It *blows out* speculators, *wipes them out, burns* them, and *kills* them with *cemetery spreads.* After a disastrous day at the exchange, traders talk about the "blood on the floor," left by a merciless market, which brought about the *October Massacres* of 1978 and 1979, and, of course, the devastating *Crash of 1929.*

The market thrives on speculators' anxieties, according to the old saying "Bull markets climb a wall of worry." It keeps Wall Streeters in a constant state of anxiety—reminding them that they cannot compete against such an unpredictable force. "The market knows," counsels another proverb, but no one can consistently wrest away what it knows. "The market is a two-way street" explains another, but no one knows which way it will turn, or when. Speculators who believe, based on temporary success in short selling, that they've succeeded in understanding the market should realize, as old-timers do, that "A swelled head is what breaks the bear."

SEX IN THE MARKETPLACE

Wall Streeters have given the market a personality through their speech. In the metaphors, the traders' attempts to dominate the market and its stocks are often sexual, with the market portrayed as a woman fighting back. Writing in 1957, Ira Glick elaborated on why commodities traders referred to the market as a whore:

> The 'market' is endowed with feminine qualities so that it is the woman; and the trader, dealing with and in the market and manipulating it by buying and selling, is the male. The 'market' is a very active woman, unpredictable, potentially treacherous, distributing and bestowing her favors capriciously.[1]

Almost thirty years later, Sonny Kleinfield found the same attitude:

> For many traders the market is a "bitch," a "cunt," a "whore," an "old lady." . . . If you "fight" it or "go up against it," chances are you'll be "screwed" by it or maybe "fucked over."[2]

Traders *straddle* the market, executing *spreads,* which are positions that have two *legs.* They pursue *in-and-out trading,* or execute market orders to *touch but not penetrate.* In the options market, Wall Streeters go *naked,* which is the opposite of *covered.* (Given the choice of "uncovered" or "naked" to describe their position, traders tend to choose the more provocative naked.)

Traders can manipulate individual stocks as well as the whole market in ways that sound sexual, by *goosing* them, *riding* them, and quickly *pulling out* of them. Numerous stock nicknames come from women's names, another way in which stocks emerge as feminine. Similarly, the old Wall Street saying "When the paddy wagon comes, they take the good girls with the bad" equates women and stocks, likening a market slump in which strong stocks fall along with the weak ones to a raid on a whorehouse. The fact that nineteenth-century Wall Streeters nicknamed Erie stock *Harlot of the Rails* and *Scarlet Woman of Wall Street* indicates that even then the interaction of speculators with stocks had sexual overtones.

ARENA OF BULLS AND BEARS

At the same time that Wall Streeters try to conquer the market, they also do battle with each other. Metaphors of physical competitions describe financial competition on Wall Street, again greatly overstating the dangers. Disagreements become wars—the *Erie Wars* fought over the *Scarlet Woman,* the *Great Alphabet War* and the *Battle of the Bulge* fought over *tombstones.*

Of all areas of Wall Street slang, the *takeover wars* convey the clearest picture of battle. *Raiders* and *white knights* come to metaphoric blows over *sleeping beauties,* while *killer bees* and *hired guns* try to *bulletproof* the targets by devising *shark repellents.* Takeover artists such as *Icahn the Terrible* and the *Gray Shark* attack with *Saturday Night Specials* and *bear hugs,* while defenders concoct *poison pills* and *bitebacks* to *scorch the earth* if need be.

The oldest image of physical competition on the street, and the one best-known to the public, pits two fierce animals against each other, a *bear* and a *bull.* In a famous statue at the New York Stock Exchange, the two beasts are locked in eternal combat, with neither one winning. Over the years, bears have banded together in *raids* and *drives* against the bulls, who in turn have done the same. In their market combats, they've *cornered, squeezed, twisted,* and *trapped* each other, in *pits* and *cockpits* and on the floor.

VIOLENCE AGAINST THE CUSTOMER

In the struggle between bull and bear, sometimes a third party, the *lambs,* takes the worst beating. The third object of domination, in addition to the market and other Wall Streeters, is the so-called *little guys,* turned into *lame ducks* and *dead ducks* by *big operators.* Again slang exaggerates by likening lack of success in the market to physical harm.

Small investors experience danger at the hands of their brokers as well as in the storms of the market, according to the metaphors. Brokers joke about sending customers away as *barefoot pilgrims,* without shoes on their feet or shirts on their backs. Among themselves, brokers mutter about *churning* annoying customers, but rarely do they *churn, burn, and bury* their clients. Though SEC staff members have dubbed brokerages *funeral parlors,* the treatment of most customers is far from lethal.

A broker who *blows a customer out after a point* makes a commission at the customer's expense, but the picture of "blowing out" surpasses the financial harm it describes. So, too, the facetiously named *alligator spread,* in which the brokers' commissions eat up the customers' profits, is hardly the equivalent of being devoured by an alligator.

Brokers verbally abuse customers because, when customers lose money, they typically blame their brokers—behavior that is far from new. Henry Fowler wrote in 1873:

> The first thing a loser in Wall Street does, after a heavy stroke
> of bad luck, is to find fault with his broker.[3]

Customers find fault with brokers who, they claim, promote worthless stocks solely for the sake of commission. As one observer put it in 1935, "A broker is a man who runs your fortune into a shoestring." But brokers, in turn, insist that customers want to hear that a stock will rise, believing thin stories out of greed. But the same customers refuse to face the reality that stocks go down as well as up, and "no tree grows to the sky," as the saying goes—no stock goes up forever.

Investors expect higher returns than a savings account offers, yet they don't want to sacrifice safety, as a 1987 survey showed. In polling investors about how much risk they were willing to take, giving choices of "no risk," "a little," "some," and "a lot," results showed that well over half of those polled chose "no risk."[4] No wonder these investors raise hell when their stocks start to sink! And no wonder brokers hold harsh opinions about customers, expressed in extreme form by William Hazlitt in 1805:

> There is no more mean, stupid, pitiful, selfish, envious, ungrateful animal than the stock-speculating public.

But since brokers, like other sales people, depend on customers for commission, they do not have the luxury of expressing themselves directly to the offending customers. They cannot afford to offend the source of their commissions, so they channel their animosity into slang and jokes that the brokers share among themselves.

PICKLES AND CROCKS

Brokers are not the only occupational group to disperse their ill-will through slang; any group that works with difficult members of the public disparages them behind their backs. Two examples of the slang of other groups, beauticians and medical personnel, illustrate attitudes similar to Wall Street's.

Beauticians, like brokers, rely on satisfied customers for their income. Also like brokers, beauticians have been expressing themselves in slang for decades. H.L. Mencken, in *The American Language*, listed the following slang terms this occupational group applied in the 1930s to their customers. *Blizzard* described a customer always in a hurry; *joe*, one who didn't tip; and *Santa Claus*, a customer who appeared only at long intervals. An elderly fat woman was a *bag* or *bitch*, and an old woman striving to look young was called *springtime*. They labeled a complaining customer a *screech*, a haughty customer *Queen Elizabeth*, and a customer with a forbidding face *a pickle*—all behind their backs, of course.[5]

Doctors and nurses—although some would deny it—currently share a lexicon of slang words to describe problem patients. They call patients feigning illness *turkeys* or *crocks*; very sick patients *trainwrecks*; dirty patients with scaly skin *lizards*; and—the most common term—dirty, chronically ill patients *gomers*.

Like Wall Streeters, medical personnel play with abbreviations. They use FLK for "Funny Looking Kid" to indicate that a child's diagnosis is not easily determined, TSTSH for "Too Sick to Send Home," and ECU for "Eternal Care Unit," where patients go when they die.[6]

The slang not only lets off steam that might otherwise be directed at the patient or customer, it also bands together the group that uses it, providing group strength for dealing with stress. In the case of Wall Streeters, the stress stems in part from anger directed at them by customers, who are frustrated when they lose money.

Often, outsiders view the medical profession as mysterious, because of its close association with life and death, and its medical jargon. Outsiders also view Wall Street as a mysterious place where important things happen concerning money; the slang and financial jargon reinforce the mystique. But when the stock market slumps and the country suffers as a result, outsiders suddenly see the mysterious aura as masking something shady.

THE PUBLIC'S PERCEPTION OF WALL STREET

Sometimes the whole country seems enamored of Wall Street, as it was in the 1920s. But, as individual customers blame their brokers when they lose money, the whole country blamed Wall Street when the market crashed in 1929. Will Rogers voiced the complaint of many Americans when he observed, "Let Wall Street have a nightmare and the whole country has to help get them back in bed again."

Although market crashes and insider trading scandals can be blamed on Wall Street, the proliferation of boiler rooms selling fraudulent stocks and commodities is not Wall Street's fault. Yet the Street's image has suffered for years because of these shady operations, which the public associates with the legitimate stock market. That the slang words and phrases of the two areas overlap highlights their similarities, indicating that the border between legitimate and illegal brokerage operators is a hazy one. Boiler-room operators and beginning brokers both spend their time *dialing for dollars,* soliciting *mooches,* and hooking *suckers.* Warnings to the public against boiler rooms no doubt make some consumers wary of all stock pitches over the telephone. The nicknames for the SEC of *Watchdog* and *Policeman* stem from and perpetuate Wall Street's image as untrustworthy, even criminal.

One of the accusations a disgruntled public hurls at the market is that buying and trading stocks or commodities is no better than gambling, an accusation made in strong terms by Theodore Roosevelt in 1908:

> There is no moral difference between gambling at cards or in lotteries or on the race track and gambling in the stock-market.

As history shows, various forms of gambling have long been linked with the stock market. For example, during the first fifty years of organized trading in New York, exchange members sold lottery tickets and took bets on sporting events or political elections.

Futures and options trading have especially suffered from associations with gambling. When exchanges introduced trading on stock market index futures, even some within the industry suggested that the new instrument might violate gambling laws. That the large British bookmaking firm Ladbrokes of London had been accepting bets for years on the Dow Jones Industrial Average seemed too close for comfort to the new futures.

Although exchange officials would flinch at the admission, most Wall Streeters would agree, at least in private, that gambling and stock speculating are not so far apart. Images in their own slang confirm this notion. No stock market term is better known to the public than *blue chip,* borrowed from poker, a metaphor the Street has extended to come up with *pale blue chip* and *white chip.* *Taking a flier* or *flutter* is general slang for taking a gamble or chance, while *hedging*—which glossaries list as a stock market term as early as 1903—is associated in the minds of many with the phrase "hedging your bets." Wall Streeters call speculation in options *rolling the bones,* from general slang for rolling dice.

Touts and *tipsters, pikers* and *punters* have all hung out at racetracks as well as on Wall Street. Terms heard on the Street such as **market players, playing the market, high-stakes game,** and **high-return market play** further the notion that buying and selling securities is a game of chance.

WALL STREET'S INFERIORITY COMPLEX

When the public turns against Wall Street, Wall Streeters react as a group by defending themselves and by returning the hostility. At the same time, their self-image suffers; for example, as the *Wall Street Journal* reported on March 9, 1987, during the insider trading scandals:

> All over the country, the sound of Wall Street hotshots not bragging about their jobs is deafening. One of them recalls a painful moment on a recent ski vacation when his chairlift-mate asked him what he did. "For the first time in ten years in this business, I was ashamed to admit I'm an investment banker," he said.

To bolster their image, Wall Streeters defend their work by saying that the markets are necessary for forming public corporations, for providing the liquidity that makes people willing to invest, and for shouldering various risks in the futures markets. Yet a feeling prevails among many Wall Streeters that they do little except push around money and take a cut of it. Comments such as "Never have so many made so much for doing so little" echo throughout Wall Street.

In a culture where the Protestant work ethic still has a wide following, skepticism prevails about the jobs of brokers, traders, and investment bankers, in which money appears to be made out of nowhere, without creating a product or contributing anything tangible to society. "All the speculation in the world never raised a bushel of wheat," observed a critic of the commodities market in 1912. In his study, Glick found that traders themselves felt that their money was "not as respectable as money made in more basic, established, secure, and overtly work oriented businesses and professions."[7]

When John Brooks explored the topic of guilt among brokers, writing about the work of the Wall Street Ministry—a religious organization run by Francis Huntington, which conducted seminars and interviews with brokers—he concluded:

> The picture that emerged from [the brokers'] talks, in 1967 and
> 1968, was of a brokerage industry ridden with guilt and frustra-
> tion. The Oxford Dictionary tells us that between the years
> 1377 and 1694 the word "broker" meant, among other things,
> "a procurer, pimp, bawd, a pander generally." To judge from
> what Huntington and his colleagues heard, many brokers in
> Wall Street in the late nineteen sixties felt its meaning hadn't
> changed very much.[8]

The primary cause of guilt was churning; brokers felt under pressure to increase their commissions and the firms profits at the customers' expense.

The jokes scattered throughout this book show that Wall Streeters are sensitive to their poor public image. The Dear Abby letter, the "my brother is a bond salesman" joke, the punch line "There are some things even a pig won't do," and other jabs Wall Streeters take at themselves are at odds with the confident stance they cultivate in public.

The public's attitude and the Wall Streeters' self-doubts leave the occupational group feeling small instead of big, insecure instead of important. To hide this insecurity, they overcompensate in slang, suppressing guilt and replacing it with a picture of power. Wall Streeters inflate their egos by populating their world with strong figures: *big operators, big producers, kings, emperors, bears, bulls, strong hands.* The public, which threatens their ego, they minimize in slang: *little guys, weak sisters, weak hands.* The only time the public is big is in the Bigger Fool Theory.

The joke about the uncultured broker who, in one version, replies to the question, "What do you think of Voltaire?" with the answer, "I figure it will go up," points to another image problem Wall Streeters have—that they are illiterate or uneducated, that a life spent making money must be uncouth. This belief has been voiced over the years in insults such as Oscar Wilde's "With an evening coat and a white tie, even a stockbroker can gain a reputation for being civilized."

To be at the top of the financial ladder may still leave a Wall Streeter with a sense of inadequacy, no matter how much a person outwardly equates self worth with net worth. Ivan Boesky, admired and envied as the wealthy **King of the Arbs** before his fall, apparently felt the need to clothe himself in academic credentials. His favorite place to do business was the Harvard Club, which he joined not as a Harvard alumnus but by giving money to the school. The jacket of his 1985 book *Merger Mania* and promotional brochures for a new arbitrage fund boasted that Boesky was serving as adjunct professor at Columbia University, a claim that Columbia denied.

MONEY AS DIRT

Wall Streeters share with the public doubts about whether the work on Wall Street is a civilized, legitimate pursuit. Judging from the slang, they also share with the rest of America an ambivalence toward the main focus of the Street: money. Undoubtedly, Americans admire and strive for wealth, and Wall Street's role as the country's leading symbol of money accounts for much of its mystique. But an analysis of the metaphors about money reveals that, while Americans pursue the almighty dollar, at the same time they unconsciously perceive it as dirty. Since the slang about money that Wall Streeters use converges with general slang about money, it is evident that the two groups share the same uneasy feeling about wealth.

In the pictures drawn by slang, losing money makes the loser clean. The victim of financial loss **takes a bath, takes a cleaning,** goes **through the financial wringer,** or gets **taken to the cleaners.** He is **cleaned out** or **wiped out,** with all the unclean money removed. At a stock market **laundry,** the person swindled got "a good cleaning"; the purpose of the **laundry business** was for the **launderer** to take money out of the market and out of the pockets of gullible investors. **Washing the market** or executing **wash sales** also took money out of the market, illegally. The person who **cleans up** from these ventures leaves the market "cleaner," as he walks away with the cash.

Of course, money obtained illegally is the dirtiest, and needs to be **laundered,** channeled through several financial institutions to make it look legitimate. But it seems all money is dirty; that's why someone with a lot of money is *filthy rich*, in general slang, and why money is *filthy lucre*. Freud drew an equation between money and feces, also found in the old proverb "Money, like dung, does no good till 'tis spread," an equation which appears to hold sway among Americans.

Whatever the psychological roots of associating money with dirt, the consequences for Wall Street are that both the public and the Street's inhabitants have a divided attitude—a love-hate affair with money. It's not surprising, in light of this, that making money is not enough, that it leaves Wall Streeters as a group feeling inadequate and even defensive.

RECHANNELING ANXIETY

Associated with dirty money, distrusted by the public, battered by the market and by each other, Wall Streeters lead lives fraught with anxiety. The unpredictability of the market causes constant worry about which way it will go and how to trade. Even taking a breather from trading may offer no relief. As a stock market maxim says, "There's more anxiety in being *out* of a market that's going up than being *in* a market that's going down."

But anxiety quickly turns to exhilaration when things go right, and both emotions overflow into humor and wordplay. The tension and high pace of Wall Street make it a hotbed for slang. With their sharpened verbal skills, Wall Streeters draw on rhyme and rhythm, humor including puns, and all varieties of figurative language. **Long and wrong, fill and kill, dialing and smiling,** and *rage in the cage* enliven their speech. Puns range from *tape-worms* to *Marilyn Monroe, sandwich spread* to *Love 'em and Leave 'em. Fried eggs, bedbug letter, lobby lizard,* and *ticker-hound* evoke a smile or laugh.

Most of all, figures of speech add sparkle to the Wall Street language—*blue-sky laws, sunshine trades, fallen angels, witching hours, poison pills.* Without consciously setting out to do so, Wall Streeters enrich the language with their slang, all the while rechanneling their tension and entertaining themselves. With the words and phrases they use every day, Wall Streeters convey their emotions and portray their flawed but always colorful world.

Notes

Chapter 1

1. Philip Hone, *The Diary of Philip Hone*, ed. Allan Nevins, vol. 2 (New York: Dodd, Mead, 1927), p. 707.
2. James Medbery, *Men and Mysteries of Wall Street*. (Boston: Fields, Osgood, & Co., 1871), p. 138.
3. *San Francisco Chronicle*, May 4, 1983.
4. Everett Mattlin, "Are the Nifty Fifty Back to Stay?" *Institutional Investor*, August 1980, p. 29.
5. "Story Time," *Newsweek*, March 6, 1972, p. 62.
6. *Time*, July 25, 1960, p. 65.
7. George Goodman, *The Wheeler Dealers* (New York: Bantam Books, 1960), p. 139.
8. Will Rogers, *Daily Telegrams*, ed. James M. Smallwood. (Stillwater, OK: Oklahoma State University Press, 1979), vol. 3, p. 150.
9. Montgomery Rollins, *Stocks and Their Market-places* (Boston: Dana Estes & Co., 1911), p. 207.
10. A. Kustomer, *P.S. What Do You Think of the Market?* (New York: Guenther Publishing, 1919), p. 10.
11. Alan Lechner, *Street Games* (New York: Playboy Paperbacks, 1980), pp. 87–88.
12. *Men and Idioms of Wall Street*. (New York: John Hickling and Company, 1875), pp. 43–44.
13. *The New York Times*, March 24, 1986.

Chapter 2

1. Kustomer, *What Do You Think*, p. 26.
2. Peter Finley Dunne, *Mr. Dooley's Opinions* (New York: R. H. Russell, 1901), p. 193.
3. A. J. Wilson, *A Glossary of Colloquial, Slang and Technical Terms in Use on the Stock Exchange and in the Money Market* (New York: Wilson & Milne, 1895).
4. W. G. Cordingley, *Cordingley's Dictionary of Stock Exchange Terms* (London: Effingham Wilson, 1901).
5. Clayton S. Scott, Jr., "Corporate Nicknames in the Stock Market," *American Speech* 35:195.
6. Robert Lossing Niles, *A Short Story of the New York Stock Exchange* (Knoxville, Tenn.: Morgan Brown Press, 1916), p. 13.
7. William G. Shepherd, Wall Street, *Business Week*, July 29, 1972, p. 37.

Chapter 3

1. *The Wall Street Journal*, February 7, 1986.
2. "Men and Movements of Finance," *Moody's Magazine*, April 1910, p. 244.
3. Edwin Lefevre, *Reminiscences of a Stock Operator* (Larchmont, New York: American Research Council, 1923), pp. 59–60.
4. John Moody, *The Art of Wall Street Investing* (New York: Moody Corporation, 1906), pp. 118–20.
5. Goodman, *Wheeler Dealers*, p. 55.
6. Frank Norris, *The Pit* (New York: Grosset & Dunlap, 1902), p. 81.
7. *The New York Times*, November 18, 1984, sec. 12.
8. Stuart Berg Flexner, *Listening to America* (New York: Simon and Schuster, 1982), pp. 537–38.
9. Louis Engel and Brendan Boyd, *How to Buy Stocks*, 7th rev. ed. (New York: Bantam Books, 1982), p. 126.
10. Bob Tamarkin, *The New Gatsbys* (New York: Morrow, 1985), p. 35.
11. Benjamin Graham, *Security Analysis* (New York: McGraw-Hill, 1962).

Chapter 4

1. *Institutional Investor*, June 1987, p. 227.
2. William Worthington Fowler, *Inside Life in Wall Street* (Hartford, Conn.: Dustin, Gilman & Co., 1873), p. 85.
3. John Moody, *The Masters of Capital* (New Haven: Yale University Press, 1920), p. 93.
4. Niles, *Short Story*, p. 13.

5. Dunne, *Mr. Dooley's Opinions*, p. 187.
6. Edward Lefevre, *Wall Street Stories* (New York, 1916), p. 132; Norris, *The Pit*, p. 332.
7. Medbery, *Men and Mysteries*, p. 99.
8. Fowler, *Inside Life*, p. 321.
9. Matthew Josephson, *The Robber Barons* (New York: Harcourt, Brace, 1964), p. 312.
10. *Review of Reviews*, February 1893, p. 35.
11. Fowler, *Inside Life*, p. 126.
12. Henry Clews, *Twenty-eight Years in Wall Street* (New York: J. S. Ogilvie, 1888), pp. 439, 444.
13. Clews, *Twenty-eight Years*, p. 441.
14. Richard D. Wyckoff, *Wall Street Ventures and Adventures* (New York: Harper and Brothers, 1930), p. 50.
15. Bernard M. Baruch, *Baruch, My Own Story* (New York: Pocket Books, 1958), pp. 141, 143.
16. Clews, *Twenty-eight Years*, p. 234.
17. Rogers, *Daily Telegrams*, vol. 2, p. 91.
18. Business & Finance, *Time*, October 28, 1929, pp. 43–44.
19. Matthew Josephson, "Jolly Bear," *The New Yorker*, May 14, 1932, p. 22.

Chapter 5

1. *Men and Idioms*, p. 7.
2. Matthew Hale Smith, *Twenty Years Among the Bulls and Bears of Wall Street* (New York: American Book Co., 1871), p. 70.
3. Lewis Owen, *How Wall Street Doubles My Money Every Three Years* (New York: Manor Books, 1969), p. 273.
4. Rollins, *Stocks and Their Market-places*, p. 202.
5. Albert W. Atwood, "Men and Markets," *The Saturday Evening Post*, April 27, 1929, p. 100.
6. Murray Bloom, *Rogues to Riches* (New York: Putnam, 1971), p. 174.
7. Smith, *Twenty Years*, pp. 69–70.
8. Norman D. Moore, *Dictionary of Business Finance and Investment* (New York: Investor's Systems, 1975), p. 489.
9. Norris, *The Pit*, pp. 88, 252.
10. J. L. Dillard, *American Talk* (New York: Random House, 1976), p. 65.
11. *Stock Market Quotations* "From the Works of Sophronia Tibbs, Collected by Leonard Hatch" (New York: John Day Co., 1926), p. 6.
12. Kustomer, *What Do You Think*, p. 16.
13. *Moody's Magazine*, February 1910, p. 82.

Chapter 6

1. *The Wall Street Journal*, December 20, 1985.
2. Alexandra Marshall, *Tender Offer* (New York: Playboy Paperbacks, 1981), p. 196.
3. William G. Flanagan, *The Takers* (New York: Bantam, 1984), p. 120.
4. William Safire, "On Language," *The New York Times Magazine*, January 27, 1985, p. 12.

Chapter 7

1. Rollins, *Stocks and Their Market-places*, p. 148.
2. *The Rogues and Rogueries of New York* (New York: J.C. Haney & Co., 1865), p. 54.
3. Smith, *Twenty Years*, p. 69.
4. Edwin Lefevre, "Stock-Market Manipulation," *The Saturday Evening Post*, February 10, 1923, p. 46.
5. Norris, *The Pit*, p. 268.
6. Norris, *The Pit*, p. 394.
7. *Men and Idioms*, p. 74.
8. Lefevre, "Stock-Market Manipulation," p. 46.
9. Eric Partridge, A *Dictionary of Slang and Unconventional English*. 8th ed. Edited by Paul Beale. (New York: Macmillan, 1984), p. 668; Albin J. Pollock, *The Underworld Speaks* (San Francisco: Prevent Crime Bureau, 1935), no pg.
10. David W. Maurer, *The Big Con* (New York: Bobbs-Merrill, 1940), p. 241.
11. Bloom, *Rogues to Riches*, p. 244.
12. Finance, *Business Week*, May 14, 1984, p. 160.
13. "Humbugs Labelled 'Business Opportunities'," *Moody's Magazine*, May 1906, p. 669.
14. Elizabeth Frazer, "Did You Lose Your Shirt in the Market?" *The Saturday Evening Post*, September 8, 1928, p. 14.

Chapter 8

1. Frazar Kirkland, *Cyclopaedia of Commercial and Business Anecdotes* (New York: D. Appleton and Co., 1868), p. 112.
2. Lefevre, *Wall Street Stories*, p. 92.
3. *Institutional Investor*, August 1969, p. 36.
4. Rollins, *Stocks and Their Market-places*, p. 14.
5. Joseph Alsop and Robert Kintner, "The Battle of the Market Place," *The Saturday Evening Post*, June 11, 1938, p. 9.

6. "N.Y. Gold Room and Stock Board," *Harper's Weekly*, October 16, 1869, p. 660.
7. Fowler, *Inside Life*, pp. 91–92.
8. Howard Irving Smith, *Smith's Financial Dictionary* (New York: n.p., 1903), p. 514; Rollins, *Stocks and Their Market-Places*, p. 183; Lester Berrey and Melvin Van Den Bark, *The American Thesaurus of Slang*. 2d ed. (New York: Thomas Y. Crowell, 1953), p. 531.
9. Medbery, *Men and Mysteries*, p. 51.

Chapter 9

1. Fowler, *Inside Life*, p. 283.
2. Louis Windmuller, "A Brief History of the Panic, and Some Lessons which It May Teach Us," *Harper's Weekly*, August 25, 1894, p. 799.
3. Will Rogers, *Daily Telegrams*, ed. by James M. Smallwood (Stillwater, OK: Oklahoma State University Press, 1978), vol. 2, p. 89.
4. Baruch, *My Own Story*, p. 135.
5. Fowler, *Inside Life*, pp. 520–21.
6. Andrew Tobias, "Elegy for a Bull Market," *Esquire*, December 5, 1978, p. 66.
7. Keeler, B. C. " 'Low' and 'High' Months," *Moody's Magazine*, June 1906, p. 38.
8. Investment and Finance, *Literary Digest*, November 24, 1928, p. 64.
9. Howard Smith, *Financial Dictionary*, p. 401.
10. Peter Finley Dunne, *Mr. Dooley Says* (New York: Charles Scribner, 1910), pp. 61, 64.

Chapter 10

1. Ira Oscar Glick, *A Social Psychological Study of Futures Trading*, Ph.D. dissertation (University of Chicago, 1957), p. 128.
2. Sonny Kleinfield, *The Traders* (New York: Holt, Rinehart and Winston, 1983), pp. 109–110.
3. Fowler, *Inside Life*, p. 261.
4. *The Wall Street Journal*, May 12, 1987.
5. H. L. Mencken, *The American Language*, Supplement Two (New York: Knopf, 1948), pp. 737–39.
6. Victoria George and Alan Dundes, "The Gomer: A Figure of American Hospital Folk Speech," *Journal of American Folklore*, v. 91, 1978, pp. 568–81.
7. Glick, *Futures Trading*, p. 117.
8. John Brooks, *The Go-Go Years* (New York: Weybright and Talley, 1973), p. 219.

Bibliography

Allen, Frederick Lewis. *The Lords of Creation*. New York: Harper & Brothers, 1935.

Baruch, Bernard M. *Baruch, My Own Story*. New York: Pocket Books, 1958.

Berrey, Lester and Melvin Van Den Bark. *The American Thesaurus of Slang*. New York: Thomas Y. Crowell, 1947.

————. *The American Thesaurus of Slang*. 2nd ed. New York: Thomas Y. Crowell, 1953.

Bithell, Richard. *A Counting-House Dictionary*. London: George Routledge & Sons, 1882.

Bloom, Murray. *Rogues to Riches*. New York: Putnam, 1971.

Brooks, John. *The Go-Go Years*. New York: Weybright and Talley, 1973.

————. *The Seven Fat Years*. New York: Harper & Brothers, 1958.

————. *Once in Golconda*. New York: Harper & Row, 1969.

Clews, Henry. *Twenty-eight Years in Wall Street*. New York: J. S. Ogilvie, 1888.

The Compact Edition of the Oxford English Dictionary. 2 vols. Oxford: Oxford University Press, 1971.

Cordingley, W. G. *Cordingley's Dictionary of Stock Exchange Terms*. London: Effingham Wilson, 1901.

Crow, William Henry. *Corporation Secretary's Guide*. New York: Prentice-Hall, 1926.

Darvas, Nicolas. *Wall Street, the Other Las Vegas*. New York: Lyle Stuart, 1964.

Dillard, J. L. *American Talk*. New York: Random House, 1976.

Dresden, Don. "Mops and Cools: In Such Terms Over-the-Counter Men Buy and Sell Securities." *The New York Times Magazine*, October 20, 1946.

Engel, Louis, and Brendan Boyd. *How to Buy Stocks*. 7th rev. ed. New York: Bantam Books, 1982.

Flanagan, William G. *The Takers*. New York: Bantam, 1984.

Flexner, Stuart Berg. *Listening To America*. New York: Simon and Schuster, 1982.

Fowler, William Worthington. *Inside Life in Wall Street*. Hartford, Conn.: Dustin, Gilman & Co., 1873.

Glick, Ira Oscar. *A Social Psychological Study of Futures Trading*. Ph.D. dissertation, University of Chicago, 1957.

Goodman, George. *The Wheeler Dealers*. New York: Bantam Books, 1960.

Hirsch, Paul M. "Ambushes, Shootouts, and Golden Parachutes." Paper in progress. Graduate School of Business, University of Chicago, 1982. Photocopy.

Hoffman, Paul. *The Dealmakers*. Garden City, N.Y.: Doubleday, 1984.

Holbrook, Stewart H. *The Age of the Moguls*. Garden City: Doubleday, 1953.

"I Got an Interpreter to Help Me Understand My Husband." *American Magazine*, July 1929.

"Jargon: Talk in Wall Street Where Bulls Feast on Melons." *Newsweek*, July 4, 1936.

Jensen, Michael C. "Takeovers: Folklore and Science." *Harvard Business Review* 62, November-December 1984.

Josephson, Matthew. *The Robber Barons*. New York: Harcourt, Brace, 1964.

Kleinfield, Sonny. *The Traders*. New York: Holt, Rinehart and Winston, 1983.

Lampert, Hope. *Behind Closed Doors*. New York: Atheneum, 1986.

———. *Till Death Do Us Part*. New York: New American Library, 1983.

Lechner, Alan. *Street Games*. New York: Playboy Paperbacks, 1980.

Lefevre, Edwin. *Reminiscences of a Stock Operator*. Larchmont, New York: American Research Council, 1923.

Lipton, Martin, and Erica H. Steinberger. *Takeovers and Freezeouts*. New York: Law Journal Seminars-Press, 1978.

Loomis, C. Grant. "Proverbs in Business." *Western Folklore* 22, 1964.

Mackay, Charles. *Memoirs of Extraordinary Popular Delusions*. Vol. 1. Philadelphia: Lindsay and Blakiston, 1950.

Maurer, David W. *The Big Con*. New York: Bobbs-Merrill, 1940.

———. *Language of the Underworld*. Edited by Alan W. Futrell and Charles B. Wordell. Lexington: University Press of Kentucky, 1981.

Mayer, Martin. *Wall Street: Men and Money*. New York: Harper & Brothers, 1955.

McNaughton, Bruce. "Basic Bull and Bear." *The New York Times Magazine*, March 13, 1955.

Medbery, James K. *Men and Mysteries of Wall Street*. Boston: Fields, Osgood, & Co., 1871.

Men and Idioms of Wall Street. New York: John Hickling and Company, 1875.

Mencken, H. L. *The American Language*. 4th ed. New York: Knopf, 1936. *Supplement One*, 1945. *Supplement Two*, 1948.

Miller, Lowell. "Is the S.E.C. Selling Wall Street Short?" *The New York Times Magazine*, April 23, 1978.

Minton, Arthur. "The Muse of Mammon." *American Speech* 24, 1949.

Moody, John. *The Art of Wall Street Investing*. New York: Moody Corporation, 1906.

———. *The Masters of Capital*. New Haven: Yale University Press, 1920.

Moore, Norman D. *Dictionary of Business, Finance and Investment*. New York: Investor's Systems, 1975.

Neill, Humphrey B. *The Inside Story of the Stock Exchange*. New York: B.C. Forbes & Sons, 1950.

Norris, Frank. *The Pit*. New York: Grosset & Dunlap, 1902.

Osborn, A. S. J. *The Stock Exchange*. London: Broad St. Press, n.d.

Partridge, Eric. *A Dictionary of Slang and Unconventional English*. 8th ed. Edited by Paul Beale. New York: Macmillan, 1984.

Pessin, Allan H. and Joseph A. Ross. *More Words of Wall Street*. Homewood, IL: Dow Jones-Irwin, 1986.

———. and Joseph A. Ross. *Words of Wall Street*. Homewood, Ill.: Dow Jones-Irwin, 1983.

Phalon, Richard. *The Takeover Barons of Wall Street*. New York: Putnam, 1981.

Pollock, Albin J. *The Underworld Speaks*. San Francisco: Prevent Crime Bureau, 1935.

Pratt, Sereno S. *The Work of Wall Street*. New York: D. Appleton & Co., 1916.

Rogers, Will. *Daily Telegrams*. Vol. 2. Ed. by James M. Smallwood. Stillwater, OK: Oklahoma State University Press, 1978. Vol. 3, 1979.

Rollins, Montgomery. *Stocks and Their Market-places*. Boston: Dana Estes & Co., 1911.

Sachs, Emanie. *The Terrible Siren*. New York: Harper & Brothers, 1928.

Sarnoff, Paul. *Wall Street Wisdom*. New York: Pocket Books, 1965.

Scott, Clayton S., Jr. "Corporate Nicknames in the Stock Market." *American Speech* 35, 1960.

Smith, Adam. *The Money Game*. New York: Random House, 1967.

Smith, Howard Irving. *Smith's Financial Dictionary*. New York: n.p., 1903.

Smith, Matthew Hale. *Sunshine and Shadow in New York*. Hartford, Conn.: J. B. Burr and Co., 1869.

———. *Twenty Years Among the Bulls and Bears of Wall Street*. New York: American Book Co., 1871.

Sobel, Robert. *N.Y.S.E.* New York: Weybright and Talley, 1975.
——. *The Big Board.* New York: Free Press, 1965.
——. *Inside Wall Street.* New York: Norton, 1977.
Sparling, Earl. *Mystery Men of Wall Street.* New York: Greenberg, 1930.
Spooner, John D. *Sex and Money.* Boston: Houghton-Mifflin, 1985.
Stinson, R. J. "Wall Street Folklore: Fact or Fancy?" *Financial World,* January 9, 1974.
Stoddard, William Leavitt. *Financial Racketeering and How to Stop It.* New York: Harper & Brothers, 1931.
Tamarkin, Bob. *The New Gatsbys.* New York: Morrow, 1985.
Taylor, John. *Storming the Magic Kingdom.* New York: Knopf, 1987.
Wentworth, Harold and Stuart Berg Flexner, eds. *Dictionary of American Slang.* 2d suppl. ed. New York: Thomas Y. Crowell, 1975.
Williamson, Ellen. *Wall Street Made Easy.* Garden City, N.Y.: Doubleday, 1965.
Wilson, A. J. *A Glossary of Colloquial, Slang and Technical Terms in Use on the Stock Exchange and in the Money Market.* New York: Wilson & Milne, 1895.
Wyckoff, Peter. *Dictionary of Stock Market Terms.* New York: Popular Library, 1964.
Wyckoff, Richard D. *Wall Street Ventures and Adventures.* New York: Harper and Brothers, 1930.

Index

Acapulco spread, 24
Admiral Fisk, 73
Aged fails, 157
Airedale, 53
Ali Baba, 149
All the eighths, 96
Alley, the, 144
Alley waddlers, 55
Alligator spread, 24, 184
Amex, 147
Angel, 104
Arbs, 107
Arena of the bears and bulls, 59
Aunt Jane, 48

Babson Break, 168
Baby bond, 19
Baby bull, 58–59
Back office, 157
Bagged, 94–95
Bagging the Street, 95
Bag-holders, 94
Bailing out, 90
Baited, 50
Ballooning a stock, 126
Bangers, 91
Banging the market, 91
Banker-Poet, The, 67

Banker's Panic, 178–79
Barefoot pilgrim, 49, 52, 184
Bargain counter, 56; hunters, 19, 56
Barnum of Wall Street, 72
Battle of the Bulge, 13, 183
Bear, 57–59, 183; campaigns, 59; cliques, 59; crowd, 59; dance, 59; drives, 59; hug, 102, 110–11, 183; market, 58; of stocks, 57; panic, 59; pools, 59; raids, 59; spread, 23; squeeze, 59; trap, 59
Beard, 107
Bearing the market, 59
Bear-skin jobbers, 58
Bedbug letter, 161, 192
Bells and whistles, 5, 20
Bellwether, 11
Bet-A-Million, 78, 79, 167
Bewitching Brokers, 74
Big Bang, 173
Big Board, 146
Big con game, 133
Big operators, 60, 184, 189
Big producer, 60, 189
Big store, the, 135
Bill and Mary Show, The, 118

Bird dog, 133
Bisexual offer, 103
Bishop of Wall Street, 143
Biteback, 118, 183
Black book, 112
Black Friday, 72, 169–71
Black knights, 104
Black Monday, 165–66
Black Saturday, 172
Black shoe, 16
Black Thursday, 167–68, 179
Black Tuesday, 166, 168, 179
Black Wednesday, 166–67, 179
Blind 'em and Rob 'em, 159
Blind pool, 125
Blip, 97
Blitzkreig tender offer, 109
Block trades, 97
Bloody Thursday, 168–69
Blow it off, 90
Blown out, 94, 181
Blowout, 14
Blow out after a point, 90, 184
Blow out a position, 90
Blue-chip raid, 103
Blue-chip stocks, 10–11, 18, 187
Blue Monday, 163–65, 177
Blue Monday syndrome, 164
Blue Room, 146
Blue-skied, 161
Blue-sky laws, 161, 192
Bob-tail pool, 125
Body rain, 119
Boiler room, 49, 50, 130–33, 186
Bootstrap bust-ups, 111
Bottom fishing, 86–87
Boutique indexes, 20
Boutiques, 158
Boxing, 93
Boy Plunger, 55, 82
Bracketing, 13
Broke a corner, 127
Broken lot, 48
Brought to the altar, 103

Bubble, 87–88
Bubble acts, 87
Bubble companies, 87
Buccaneers, 104
Bucket, to, 130
Bucket shops, 130–31
Bulge bracket, 13
Bull, 57–59, 183
Bull campaigns, 59
Bull cliques, 59
Bull contingent, 59
Bulletproof, 111, 112, 183
Bulling the market, 59
Bulling the prices, 59
Bullish, 58
Bull market, 58
Bull pen, 157
Bull pools, 59
Bull raids, 59
Bull runs, 59
Bull spread, 23
Bull trap, 59
Bureau of Missing Persons, 158
Burned, 94, 181
Bust-up artists, 111
Butterfly spread, 24
Buttonwood Tree Agreement, 145

Call, 21, 91
Camomail, 117
Capping, 137–38
Captain Swift, 67
Casual pass, 108
Cats and dogs, 10, 12
Caught in a corner, 126
Caught short, 92
Cemetery spread, 24–25, 181
Charlie Vapor, 67
Chasing the market, 86
Cheapo Charlie, 159
Chinaman, The, 53
Chinese Wall, 157–58
Churchyard & Graves, 160
Churn, burn and bury, 136, 184

Churning, 136–37, 184, 189
Cleaned out, 94
Clean up, to, 95, 190
Clipped, 52, 191
Cliques, 125
Closet indexers, 98
Club, the, 145
Coal Hole, 149
Coat-tail the market, 56
Cockpit, 149, 183
Cocksy, 132
Combinations, 125
Comex, 151
Commodore's pups, 74
Commodore Vanderbilt, 73
Concepts, 9
Contrarians, 62, 63
Coolidge Boom, 175
Cooling-off period, 14
Cooling period, 14
Copper a tip, 99
Corned Beef with Lettuce, 159
Corner, 126–28, 183
Corporate marriage broker, 103
Costa Rica hedge, 24–25
Coupon clippers, 18
Covered, 21, 182
Covering their shorts, 92
Coxey, 132
Crack spread, 24
Crash of 1929, 166, 179, 181
Creeping control campaign, 108
Creeping tender, 108
Cross, 97
Crowd, 146
Crown jewel option, 114–15
Curb, the, 147
Curb stocks, 147
Curbstone brokers, 147
Customer's ladies, 53
Customer's man, 52
Customer's women, 53
Cuts the melon, 17
Cyanide capsule, 116

Damsel in distress, 105
Darvas Boom, 177
Deacon, The, 71
Dead duck, 54–55, 183
Department Store of Finance, 158
Dewey, Scruem & Howe, 137
Dialing and smiling, 50, 191
Dialing for dollars, 157, 187
Diamond Jim, 78, 79
Digest, 14
Dimes, 96
Disco brokers, 159
Discos, 33
Distress sales, 91
Dr. Gloom, 65
Dr. Smooth, 67
Dog, 10
Doomsday pill, 116
Doubled-barreled, 109
Double triple witching hour, 172
Downtick, 96
Dress up portfolios, 98
Dumb money, 60
Dumping, 91, 181
Dynamiters, 133

Eat the stock, 94
Eighth-chasers, 56, 181
Eisenhower Boom, 176
Eisenhower Bull Market, 176
Elders, 148
Elephants, 97
Erie Castle, 73
Erie Wars, 71, 183
Evergreen prospectus, 14
Expiration Friday, 171–72

Fails, 157
Fallen angels, 11, 192
Fancies, 6
Fancy stocks, 6
Father of Puts and Calls, 77
Favorite Fifty, 8
Felix the Fixer, 64

Fill or kill order, 86, 181, 191
Financial supermarkets, 158
Financial wringer, 99, 190
Fix, the, 134
Fleece, to, 52
Flight to quality, 98
Flipover, 116
Flippers, 16
Flipping, 15–16
Floated, 12
Floating stock, 12
Floor, the, 157
Floor animals, 61
Flotation, 12
Flower, 5, 19
Flower bonds, 19
Flyer, 10
Fly high, 10
FOB, 159
Foreign shares, 149
Forty thieves, 149
Free-riders, 15, 17
Freezeout, 119
Fried eggs, 96, 192
From womb-to-tomb, 158
Front call, 132
Fronter, 132
Front-loaded, 109
Front-money, 53
Front running, 137, 138
Frozen account, 89
Fundamentalists, 62
Funeral parlors, 161, 184
Futures contracts, 20

Garage, the, 146
Get in on the ground floor, 86
Ghost stocks, 11
Gilt-edged, 19
Give-up, 98
Glamour stock, 5, 7–8
Glove sizes, 97
Go-go brokers, 53; funds, 53; managers, 53; stock, 53

Go private, 119; public, 15; south, 94
Go to the wall, 94
Gold Room, 149
Gold-Paved Street, 142
Goldbugs, 149
Golden Canyon, 142
Golden handcuffs, 119; handshake, 119; parachute, 118–19
Goldman Slacks, 159
Goldy, 159
Gone out the window, 14
Gone south, 94
Goodbye kiss, 117
Goose job, 88
Goosing the bowl, 88
Goosing the market, 88, 182
Grant & Ward Crash, 69, 178
Gray Acquisitor, 106
Gray knight, 106
Gray Shark, 106, 183
Great Alphabet War of 1976, 13, 183
Great American Reindeer, 156
Great Bear of Wall Street, 70
Great Man, 78
Greenmail, 108, 117–18
Greenmailers, 117
Green shoe option, 16
Growth stock, 5, 8
Gunning a stock, 126
Gunslinger, 53–54, 181
Gutter market, 147
Guttersnipes, 147

Hammering, 91, 181
Handkerchief trick, 71
Harlem Squeeze, 93
Heart Attack Market, 176
Hedge, 89, 187
Hemline theory, 100
High-flier, 5, 10
High-return market play, 188

High stakes game, 188
High steppers, 7
Hipshooter, 53–54, 181
Hired guns, 111, 183
Hit the bid, to, 90, 181
Hog, 55
Holding the baby, 94
Holding the bag, 94
Hot-air specialties, 126
Hot issue, 14
Hot stuff, 13, 132
House on the Corner, 77
House that Bellies Built, 151
Houses, 157
Hushmail, 117

Icahn the Terrible, 117, 183
In-and-out traders, 56, 182
Inside dope, 139
Inside information, 139–41
Insideman, 135
Insider, 60
Insider training, 120–22, 138–41, 161
Irish-American Exchange, 147
Irish dividend, 17
Irv the Liquidator, 65
Ivan the Pig, 65

Jacked up, 127
Jacks, 39
Jackscrewed, 127, 181
January effect, 174
Jaws, 65
Jay Cooke Panic, 178
Jellyroll spread, 24
Jesus Christ and his Twelve Apostles, 77
Jewish dentist defense, 115
Jiggle, 160–61
Joe Granville Day, 177–78
Johnson Bull Market, 177
Jubilee Jim, 72
Junior securities, 17

Junk, 19
Junk Bond King, 65
Junk bonds, 19
Junk heap, 19
Jupiter, 77

Kennedy Bull Market, 176–77
Kickers, 20
Kidder Nobody, 159
Killer bees, 111, 183
Killing, 17, 95, 181
King Jack, 67
King of the Arbs, 121, 190; of the Bears, 82; of the Bucket Shops, 67; of the Speculators, 82; of the Takeovers, 115; of Wall Street, 70
Knife, 151

Lady Brokers, 74
Ladybulls, 53
Lamb, 49, 52, 183
Lame duck, 54–55, 75, 183
Lame duck exchange, 55
Lane of the Ticker, 156
Last frontier, 151
Laugh, 96
Launderer, 129, 191
Laundering money, 129
laundry, 129, 190
Lay Back & Whack It, 160
Lifting a leg, 23
Lily, 49, 52
Literary counterattack, 113
Little Bitters, 66
Little Board, 146
Little Napoleon of the Railroads, 69
Little Wizard of Wall Street, 69
Load call, 133
Lobby lizards, 47, 192
Lobby rats, 47
Lobster, The, 66
Locked in, 89
Lock-up, 115

Lollipop, 116
Long, 57, 86
Long and wrong, 86
Louis the Sixteenth, 67

McKinley Market, 175
Mad Austrian, 65
Maiden, 105
Mark, 134, 135
Married put, 21
Match King, 81–82
May Day, 173
Melon, 17
Melon cutting, 17
Mephistopheles of Wall Street, 71
Merc, 151
Merger King, 65
Merger mania, 119, 181
Mighty Mouse of Block Trading, 64
Milking the Street, 125–26
Mr. Wall Street, 65
MOB spread, 24
Money King of Wall Street, 76
Money-washing, 129
Monk of Wall Street, 121
Mooch, 132, 187; man, 133; manna, 133
Morganization, 77
Morse Panic, 178
Mudhens, 53
Mullet, 49–51
Munis, 24

Naked, 21, 182
Naked option writers, 21
Napoleon of LaSalle Street, 68
Napoleon of the Exchange, 69
Napoleon of the Public Board, 69
Napoleon of the Street, 68
Needlemen, 132, 133
New issue fever, 15, 181
New issue-itis, 15
Nickels, 96
Nifty Fifty, 8

NOB spread, 24
No-brainer, 97

October Massacre, 172–73, 181
Odd lot, 48
Odd-lot public, 48
Off-board, 154
O'Hare spread, 24–25
Oil patch, 113
Old Board, 149
Old Eighty Millions, 74
Old guard, 148
Old Hutch, 67
Old Hutch Panic, 67
OTC, 154, 155
Out-of-the-money, 22
Outsiders, 48
Overhangs, 14
Over the counter, 154

Pac-Man strategy, 118
Pad-shovers, 156
Painting the tape, 129
Pale blue chip, 5, 11, 187
Panic, 178
Panic of 1929, 179
Paper, 132
Parent company, 17
Paying ransom, 117
P-Coast, 150
Penny-stockitis, 10
Penny stocks, 10
Performance funds, 8
Performance stock, 5, 8
Petit Bang, Le, 173
Phantom stocks, 11
Pierpontifex Morgan, 77
Pig, 55
Piggy, 65
Piker, 56, 187
Pin-striped pork bellies, 21
Pirates, 104
Pits, 151, 183
Pit traders, 152

Plain vanilla, 20
Platinum parachute, 119
Play for a point, 90
Play the market, 86, 188
Plier, 133
Pluck the chicken, to, 133
Plum, 17
Plunger, 55
Plus-tick, 97
Plus-tick rule, 97
Pocket-Book Jimmie, 67
Pointer, 99
Poisoned tips, 56
Poison pill, 115–16, 183, 192
Policeman at the Corner of Wall
    and Broad, 161, 187
Pools, 124–25
Porcupine defenses, 112
Pork bellies in pin stripes, 21
Position trader, 61
Pounding, 91
Predators' ball, 160
Prince of Erie, 73
Pru Bache, 159
Puff, 99
Punter, 56, 187
Pup, 10
Pure plays, 86
Puts, 21
Pyramiding, 87

Quack, 96
Queens of Finance, 75
Quick & Dirty, 159

Radio Fever, 175
Rag, the, 134–36
Rage in the cage, 157, 192
Raiders, 103, 104, 183
Random Walk, 62–63
Razz, 131
Red herring, 14
Reloader, 133
Rich man's panic, 179

Ride a stock, 86, 182
Rig the market, 123–24, 161
Rings, 125
Roast Beef Rare, 66
Rolling the bones, 187
Roper, 135
Rothschild Rule, 86
Round lot, 48
Round trip, 85
Running for the hills, 90
Running to cover, 92

Saddles the market, 91
Safe harbor, 112
Safe haven, 112
Salting them down, 88
Sand-bagging, 112
Sandwich spread, 24, 192
Saturday Night Special, 109–10, 183
Scalper, 55
Scalping, 55–56, 137, 181
Scalping the market, 55
Scapegoat of the Crash, 81
Scorched earth defenses, 113–14,
    183
Seasoned, 11
Seat, 155
Sell 'em Ben, 83–84
Selling against the box, 93
Sell short, 57, 92
Senior securities, 17
Set afloat, 12
Sex without marriage, 103
Shadow market, 21
Shark, 102, 106
Shark repellent, 112, 183
Sheared, 52
Shifty Thrifties, 8
Shingle theory, 161
Short, 87, 91–93
Short against the box, 93
Short interest, 91–92
Short seller, 91
Short-squeeze play, 92

Showstoppers, 113
Shuts the stock down, 89
Silent Henry, 125
Silver bullets, 19
Silver Fox, 78, 79–80
Silver Thursday, 169
Singer, 132
Slamex, 159
Slaughter, 181
Sleeper, 7
Sleeping beauty, 105, 183
Smart money, 60
Smart money boys, 60
Smart money men, 60
Smoking gun, 110
Solly, 159
Sour bond, 20
Spilling, 91
Spin-off, 17
Spot market, 151
Spread-eagles, 23
Spreads, 22–25
Sputnik Market, 176
Squawk box, 158
Stag, 15
Stagging the market, 15
Stale bear, 59
Stale bull, 59
Standing on velvet, 95
Stoking the broiler, 132
Story stocks, 8
Straddles, 22, 182
Strangle, 22, 181
Straps, 22
Street, the, 72, 144–45
Street of Sorrows, 142
Street of Ticker Tape, 156
Stretch, 65
Strike price, 21–24
Strips, 22
Strong bear hug, 110–11
Strong hands, 48
Subtippees, 99
Sucker, 49–50, 187

Sucker list, 50
Sucker play, 50
Sucker rally, 50, 59
Suede-shoe boys, 133
Sugar pill, 116
Suicide pill, 116
Suitor, 103
Sunshine Charley, 81
Sunshine trade, 98, 192
Sweetener, 20
Sweetheart, 104
Switching, 136
Swung the corner, 126

Tailer, 56
Tailgating, 56–57
Tailor, 56
Take a flutter, 86, 187
Take a flier, 10, 187
Take a plunge, 55
Takem & Makem, 160
Taken to the cleaners, 94, 190
Takeover artist, 106
Takeover fever, 119
Take some gas, 94
Taking a bath, 94
Taking a cleaning, 94, 190
Taking off a leg, 23
Talent, 60
Tall Paul, 65
Tap city, 93
Tape, the, 155–56
Tape dancing, 137
Tape-watchers, 156
Tape-worms, 156, 192
Tapped out, 93
Technicians, 62
Teddy-bear pat, 108
Teenie, 96
Telling the tale, 135
Tender, 108
Tender offer, 108
Tender traps, 109
"They," 61

Thimblerigging the market, 124, 130
Third Market, 155
Threshold deterrents, 112
Thundering Herd, 158–59
Tick-by-tick, 96
Ticker-hounds, 156, 192
Tickeritis, 156
Tickerosis, 156, 181
Ticker-sense, 156
Ticker Tape Stem, 156
Ticks, 96
Tip, 99
Tip out, 93–94
Tippees, 99
Tipster sheets, 99–100
Tipsters, 99, 187
Titans of Finance, 67
Toehold purchase, 108
Tombstone, 12, 183
Touch but don't penetrate, 23, 182
Tout, 133, 137, 187
Tout sheets, 99
Trading crowd, 146
Trading on a shoestring, 87
Trading post, 146
Trading up, 98–99
Traps, 6
Triggering, 116
Triple witching hour, 171–72, 192
Tulipomania, 150–51
Turned the screws, 128
Turrible Things, 67
Twisting, 136, 183
Twisting the shorts, 92
Two-dollar broker, 61
Two-step tender, 109

Uncle Daniel, 36, 71
Uncle Dan'l, 71
Undigested, 14–15
Unloading, 90–91
Upstairs, 157
Uptick, 96–97
Uptick rule, 96–97

Ursa Major, 66
Ursa Minor, 66

Vanishing author, 115
V.D., 98
Vestal Virgins, 8, 12

Waddle out of the alley, to, 54
Wailing Wall Street, 143
Waldorf Crowd, 78
Walk-ins, 47
Wall Street, 150
Wall Street of the West, 150
Wall Street piranhas, 106
War baby, 19
War-bride boom of 1915, 19
War brides, 19
War chest, 112–13
Washed down, 129
Washed up, 129
Washing, 128–29, 191
Wash sales, 128–30, 191
Watchdog of Wall Street, 160, 187
Watching the tape, 156
Water stocks, 16
We, the People, 158
Weak hands, 48, 189
Weakly held, 48
Weak sisters, 48, 189
Western Blizzard, 178–79
White chips, 11, 187
White Elephant, 66
White knight, 104, 106, 183
White shoe, 16
Widows and orphans, 48–49
Wildcat stocks, 10
Wild Friday, 171
Winchell Market, 177
Window dressing, 98
Wings, 24
Wiped out, 93, 181, 190
Wire, the, 135
Wise money boys, 60
Witch of Wall Street, 75

Wizard of Lazard, 64
Wizard of Wall Street, 72
Wolf of Wall Street, 82–83
Wolves, 52
Wonder stocks, 7

Yackers, 132
Yaks, 132

Yo-yo stocks, 10
Young Napoleon of Finance, 68–69
Young turks, 148
Yuppie Five, 66

Zingers, 100